GW00499268

Rachel's Keys

ECH

This book is dedicated to
my Grandmother *Raquel* z'l
and to you, my dear reader

The following chapters are not the excerpts of an old diary. I write for my readers as an adult, piecing together recollections of my early life. For this task I have tried to recreate, in part, and to the best of my ability, the ways in which I thought and spoke back then. This may come across as a little strange at the beginning, but I assure you that as you read on, I will grow and the breadth of my vocabulary will grow with me. I hope that you are willing to show some patience and that the task of reading about past events in the present tense indicative mood will be an easy one. I want to clarify that this device is intentional and not a mere oversight. I have every confidence that by the end of the book you will not be disappointed.

ECH, your helpful writer.

MANY THANKS

Being grateful is one of the many teachings left to me by my grandmother Raquel. Today I conceive of it as an important virtue that can make a big difference in our lives and fill us with positive emotions.

Writing this book was not an easy task. Inconveniences frequently reared up before me and I had to exhaust all my reserves of determination to overcome them. Fortunately, help came in many forms from many wonderful people, starting with my students, who insisted I record my experiences to increase the crop of inspiration that, according to them, emerged from my life story.

I would thereby like to thank first, from the depth of my heart, the hundreds of students who over the years have taken my classes in Oxford, Jerusalem, Córdoba, Buenos Aires, San Juan, Tierra del Fuego, Berlin, Port Stanley, Salamanca and Cambridge; you were my principal motivation to carry out this work.

Finally, a special thanks to the two main engines behind the book: Sandra Erejomovich, my soul friend whose energy was contagious, forbidding me from giving up on the project, and finally Leo Sagor, my faithful companion in life, whose captivating eyes cast their sharp gaze over the final draft. It was Leo who was ever present to support me throughout, endlessly preparing me hot *mate*, the famed herbal tea of the Guaraní, keeping me awake deep into many cold Oxonian nights, offering his approval and continued enthusiasm.

To them and to all of you, my dear readers, thank you very, very much.

Esteban Cichello Hübner

PROLOGUE

"I closed the book and the world opened up to my eyes."

These simple verses of Unamuno succinctly capture the sense of attraction sparked by my reading Rachel's Keys.

Esteban, the narrator-protagonist of the book, draws out the alternating phases of human experience from a richly diverse range of perspectives. His words communicate a passionate vision of life, one that emerged despite a tough start in life, one that deeply resonated with me. Indeed, he was forced to reckon prematurely with the bitterness derived from the world's squalor.

As I progressed through his story, each chapter laid bare to me his way of looking at the world, one which though changing would always link back to the evocative words of his grandmother Raquel, the inspiration of the book.

We accompany Esteban on his own particular path of self-education. He shares with us the events that marked his childhood and youth, which forged in him an attitude of struggle and perseverance in the face of adversity. On every line we follow the moral and intellectual formation of the protagonist forever dreaming through a series of revealing moments that capture his doubts, his internal conflicts and the personal decisions that he must make, conditioned as he is by his environment of material poverty. For such occasions, however, he is fortunate enough to have the spiritual wealth inherited from his mother and Grandmother to guide him.

I would highlight the great awareness shown in the gaze of this tender and innocent child faced with such instability. I would point to the strength of his convictions as elemental in allowing him to synthesize his will to overcome himself; for in every personal choice he reaffirms his stance and continues to look to the horizon in search of his dreams.

The unique worldview that Esteban presents in the pages of Rachel's Keys shows a human being as he suffers, fights and makes choices, while harbouring every confidence in his existence: studying, working, learning languages, travelling, conquering the Obelisk and the world.

In the words of the protagonist himself: "I want to be the best player at life itself". It's a real lesson for those who feel the weight of hardship pressing down on the fragility of their dreams.

The message conveyed by Esteban is one of hope and courage:

Follow your dreams... because dreams can indeed come true.

Claudia González Sosa

Doctor in Hispanic Philology

University of Salamanca

Let us begin…

ONE
Elena
Good and dumb

Raquel passed away today. Perhaps she left this world two days ago, I'm not quite sure. On Avenida Márquez, next to the Hippodrome at San Isidro, in the Province of Buenos Aires in the Republic of Argentina, where many horses run for money, she is hit by the driver of a white Renault 12 at five-thirty in the morning. The impact propels her through the air, about seven meters, and she lands on the hard black cobblestones of the wide avenue. She left but her words still resonate within me.

I'm visiting the centre of Buenos Aires for the first time in my life; I'm over the moon and hope it won't be the last time either. It's for a school trip and, early on this Tuesday morning, at school we board a bus belonging to the company Alvarez from San Isidro. There's a whole bunch of us, Grades A and B combined, and we're accompanied by Srta. Elsa, the headmistress Elena, who always smells of mothballs, and another teacher whose name I don't know.

I'm sitting next to the headmistress in the front row of seats. It's a bit intimidating but not so much that I won't join in singing a few songs to do with the trip. One goes like this: "Chofer, chofer, apure ese motor, que en esta cafetera nos morimos de calor!" (Driver, driver, speed up the engine! We're dying of heat in this coffee pot!)

I don't really get the song. First of all, I find it disrespectful to the driver, and then there's that coffee pot thing, what's that got to do with the bus? But the second song leaves me even more perplexed, it's by a singer called Pipo Pescador and goes something like this: "Vamos de paseo, pi-pi-pi, en un auto feo, pi-pi-pi, pero no me importa, pi-pi-pi, porque llevo torta, pi-pi-pi…" (We're going for a ride, in an ugly car, but I don't care because I'm bringing cake…) But we're not in a car, we're in a bus and we don't have any cake either. Before we left, I prepared a paper bag with a tomato and mustard sandwich, a green apple and an empty bottle of water that I went to fill up in the bathroom. We're lucky to have taps with delicious fresh water at school.

This is only the second time I've left my neighbourhood in the nearly two years since I arrived here. The farthest I sometimes go is to San Isidro high street and maybe Boulogne Sur Mer. The latter has one of the weirdest town names I've come across in the Province of Buenos Aires; people pronounce it all sorts of ways: "Bulones", Bulón", "Buloññññe" and "Sur Mer". There doesn't seem to be any consensus.

As I said, I don't know the Federal Capital at all, or 'the centre', as Mum calls it, and the sweet headmistress Elena notices my face lighting up in wonder as I stare out the window. But more than just looking, I'm admiring everything I set eyes on.

Everything seems enormous and there's so much green everywhere, trees, flowers and parks. The streets are all paved with tarmac, hundreds of cars running smoothly along them. I notice that many of them are painted the same colour and look identical, yellow roof and black doors. I'm a little confused at first, but after some deep reflection I realise they must be taxis. I wonder what it's like to travel in one. It must be truly wonderful to just hop in, tell the driver to take you to a certain location and have him obey just like that. All taxi drivers wear ties and look like smart and friendly people.

The bus saunters down Avenida Libertador, the second longest avenue in the country with its almost 27 kilometres, and as it turns onto Avenida 9 de Julio, the widest in the world, I spot the Obelisk, the second tallest on the planet, and immediately stand up, right there, on my seat, rigid in amazement, and exclaim, "It's the Obelisk, ma'am!"
The headmistress looks up at me shocked and, in the tone of Sergeant Garcia, the guy from that series El Zorro, calls out, "Sit down! What's the matter? You've never been to Buenos Aires?"
"What?! I live in Buenos Aires, ma'am", I reply.
But then I quickly remember what my friend Juan Lanusse used to say whenever he was asked where his grandfather was, the president of the nation, and, embarrassed, I confess to the headmistress that this is the first time I have been to 'Buenos Aires'.

It makes me feel even worse when, to my surprise, her voice now bawling, she tells the other teachers about my lack of *capital* culture. All my schoolmates are also listening in and so the humiliation only grows. "But it's so close, only fifty minutes on the electric train Mitre!" the headmistress continues prattling.

I'd like to give her an earful, tell her that you should never humiliate anyone, let alone in front of other people. But what could I ever say to rebuke this belittling headmistress regarding my *capital* ignorance, if my own mother, who is much older than me, hasn't ever been to the centre either, let alone the underground.

The joy and euphoria quickly dissolve into humiliation and dejection. I sit there, motionless, crying inside. As the bus passes down the Diagonal Norte heading towards Plaza de Mayo, we get even closer to the majestic Obelisk and one of the other kids asks the headteacher, "Ma'am, can we get to the top?"
She responds in a dry, assured tone, "No. It's forbidden to go up the Obelisk".

At this point, I say to myself in silence, "*I'll* get up there one day, I promise you, Esteban". Then another voice in my head says, "You're going to go up there and you're going to conquer the Obelisk. You'll see." How on earth am I going to keep this self-made promise? Or is it better to do something without promising it, than to promise it and not to fulfill it?

CHAPTER TWO
Ester
Sacrified and buoyant

My mother Ester, who's name is written without an 'h' by the way, salty tears flowing freely from her sad eyes, kneels next to me, so that we are eye to eye, and tells me that her mother, my grandmother, is in very, very bad shape. I don't quite understand what it's like to be in a very, very bad shape, but my mum explains to me that as my grandma was getting out of the blue coloured bus, number 707, the one she takes every morning to travel to work at San Isidro's Public Health Care clinic, a man who was driving drunk ran her over.

She was scooped up by another car and checked in at her workplace, the hospital, and from there they took her in a large car with a bed and everything, a red light on its roof and a very loud siren. Where this car goes, I don't remember what it's called, but it's a very long word, it makes quite a din, and all the other cars give way to it as if the person inside is very famous. Little do they know it's just my grandmother. Anyway, she is transported in this van like thing for the sick to another hospital with an ugly name, the Cetrángulo, and there she remains for forty-two hours in a coma.

I don't understand what it means to be in a coma; for me a coma is just that little banana-shaped mark that you write across the line to separate sentences and allow you to breathe when you read them. I begin imagining that after the accident with the car my grandma has been left all crooked like a coma, unable to breathe and that's why she's not feeling well now.

Two days later, mum once again kneels down at my side, levelling her eyes with mine again, and tells me that life is ephemeral and that Grandma died very young at fifty-three. I don't understand that word 'ephemeral', but I don't say anything because I can see she's very upset, and also because I think that fifty-three is rather a lot.

She then tells me that Grandma is sleeping, that we'll meet her again when we die, that we'll meet her in heaven. She keeps telling me that Grandma's not coming back to us but that we're going to go to her, and that we have to be patient. I begin to cry now, feeling her absence. I don't have the patience to wait for death in order to see her again.

On June 3, before taking her off for a swift funeral in Martínez, they escort her coffin in a black car around the place she worked for 18 years as a hospital cleaner. The traders just across from the hospital all lower their blinds to show their respect. They know Raquel because she used to wash down the pavement opposite them every day, greeting everyone who passed by with a smile. "A smile costs less than electricity and produces more light," she'd always say to me.

In the proximity to the hospital it's possible to hear muffled cries of "They're bringing Raquel!" and "Here comes Raquel!". Her fellow municipal workers lined up on the pavement she had long kept clean. As the black car passes slowly in front of the building along Diego Palma street, dozens of old colleagues join behind it, not just from the hospital, but from the municipal workshop and the municipal workers' union of San Isidro. They walk silently behind the hearse showing deep respect for her.

Grandma Raquel was a Peronist. But more than that, mum says she was an "evitista"; for, like almost everyone who worked alongside her, she loved Evita Perón. The solemn farewell is presently greeted by the piercing sound of ambulance sirens, several parked at the main gate of her beloved hospital united in their lament. It's evident that she was very much loved there. A whole host of maids, cleaners, nurses and even some doctors wave at her from the side while others weep knowing that the virtuous, self-sacrificing and righteous Raquelita is leaving the hospital never to return.

For us, my grandmother's departure means that we lose our family's memories. She was the only one keeping them, and now she has left without sharing them with us.

My poor mum Ester is dismayed by her mum's death and seeing her makes me even sadder. Now at my paternal grandparents' house, I lock myself in the guest room crying over our loss and remembering the last kiss grandma Raquel gave me only two days ago.

I feel her close embrace, such a warm impression upon my childhood, and sense her words of sound advice still ringing in my ears. "Estebancito," as she used to call me, "Have no fear of any being, only God, and love your neighbour with all your heart; you must also respect your parents and teachers, and even when you feel the onset of *pesgaduras* (a word meaning that sort of heaviness of mind which stops people from doing things), never give up, keep studying, do your homework, always finish what you start, don't forget to feed the pets before you yourself have eaten, always tell the truth, don't steal, and always think about nice things. You're a good boy, I know. Though you do sometimes misbehave, you always seem to make those around you happy." The kisses she placed on my forehead are still fresh in my mind and in my heart.

By now I haven't seen my mother for three days. When the accident happened, she left me at my other Grandmother's house, my father's mother, who's alive and well. Her name is Berta, but we call her Lala, and her husband Lalo, so that no one really thinks of them as old grandparents at all. The only good to come from all the bad and sad stuff happening to us is that I'm feeling great here.

They have a big, well-built house with electricity, a mosaic floor and another one made of wood called a parquet. The floors are always spotless and polished with wax. Everyone has to put these sort of rags on their feet that Lala says prevent us from leaving marks. The freshly waxed floors have an alluring smell that makes my nose want to dance.

I love using the feet rags as skates. When no one's around, I race myself across the floor crashing into furniture, knocking myself quite hard and sometimes hitting the floor, but I never end up dead like grandma Raquel.
There is also a large black telephone in the house. Apparently it's very expensive to use. Lalo, who's actually

called Pedro Ramón, says he had to wait twenty years after ordering it for it to be connected. Sometimes he says the house was built with a loan from President Juan Perón himself, but other times he says the money was given to him by the Mortgage Bank. I don't really want to ask him to explain about who really gave him the loan because I'm afraid he'll only confuse me even more or perhaps scratch my face with the three-day beard he's always sporting. He knows I don't like him rubbing his chin on my face and I think that's why he does it: just to tease me!

I haven't had a go on the telephone yet, but I really can't wait to hear right up close the voice of someone who's far away, and hear my own voice too. Just to think you can have a conversation without seeing the other person's face seems magical to me.

However, the best thing about the house is that there are taps with running water, one for normal water and another for hot water! Besides that, they have a bathroom with a seat where you can sit down easily for a pee or poo; then all you have to do is press a button which releases lots of water to clean everything down the hole. They call it a toilet or something like that. The Lalos keep saying you have to pull the chain, but there is no chain! It's more of a button on the wall which you have to press. These adult things can really confuse me sometimes.
Most confusing of all is my grandmother Berta, who I call by her real name and not Lala as she prefers, because she's always making such a fuss about what she's doing. She

spends her time talking to other adults in a strange language called gibberish, which is very complicated and difficult to understand. But she doesn't speak gibberish on account of not knowing Spanish, she knows it very well, even though her mother Bule, that is, my great Grandmother, is German. She knows very well how to talk like me, but she chooses to speak gibberish so that neither I nor my brother Daniel can have any idea what she's talking about.

My grandpa answers her in Spanish, even though he is in fact Italian. After paying attention for a while, I manage to decipher the secret language: it involves adding the letter 'p' after every vowel, followed by the same vowel it precedes, 'café', for example, becomes *capafepe.*
Having just worked it out, I realise they're now talking about me and my mother, so I say nothing of my recently acquired skill. I think what they're doing is kind of disrespectful but I commit myself to listening in, trying to understand and, above all, keeping quiet.

The adults are sitting in the kitchen, drinking *mate* poured by my grandfather. There's a special cup with a little pipe in it called a straw and you fill it with a type of green tea, bits of leaf and stem alike, called yerba or *yerba mate*, and then pour hot water over it, known simply as hot water. Out of the mix comes a pleasant grassy aroma that makes me instantly curious to try it.

Before passing the cup to my aunt Myrtha he adds some sugar, but I notice that when he drinks, he doesn't. My grandmother doesn't drink at all; she says that *mate* is for low class people. I don't understand what she means or why *I'm* not allowed to drink it. I think that I should be allowed to taste it because I'm very short, which is like being low. Anyhow, I decide not to complain this time. I'll try it for myself when nobody's around.

In the meantime, they talk and talk. I'd prefer them to stop talking so that Lalo can make me a paper kite. It's amazing how fast he can make them combining bits of paper of different colours. He can match the kits of River Plate, Boca Juniors and San Lorenzo. He likes the colours of San Lorenzo best because it's his favourite football team. This time he makes me one to match River because my brother always makes me say I support them, but actually I prefer the colours of Talleres de Córdoba, dark blue and white, and Boca Juniors, blue and yellow. All this gets a bit confusing, but on top of that, while grandpa is making the kite, he explains to me that I'm Argentinian, although in my veins, of course, flows the blood from other faraway lands like his beloved Italy. I tell him he's completely wrong because I'm none of that, I'm just from Córdoba, plain and simple.

My aunt Myrtha is so sweet to me and I love her very much. She takes me to her house which is just behind my grandparents' house, on Calle Blas Parera, San Isidro, Province of Buenos Aires.

She explains to me that this province was not named on

account of its fine air, but because many years ago when they first founded the city they chose the name of *Santa María de los Buenos Ayres*; they then left out the first part because it was too long and wasted a lot of ink and so it's now just Buenos Aires, which also happens to be the name of the capital of Argentina.

Aunt Myrtha is always teaching me interesting things. For instance, she explains that I'm *cordobés*, because I was born in another province called Córdoba, which is full of intelligent people who are all doctors and that's why they also call it the La Docta (The Wise). She informs me that I was born in a place called La Falda. This also somewhat confuses me because La Falda means 'the skirt', or 'the lap'. When there's nowhere to sit, adults tell me, "Esteban, come sit on my lap." Do they really mean for me to sit where I was born? It makes me wonder if Mafalda, the girl from the comic strip, who's always wearing a skirt, was also born in La Falda like me. Words are weird, aren't they?

I start going to a kindergarten called Pimpollitos ('Little Buds'), only a block away from my house, to the left; later on, I go to an elementary school also a block away, but to the right. It's funny because the blocks in our neighbourhood are normal, but the one I live on is about three times longer than the rest. I walk to kindergarten in a blue-coloured coat with small chequers that was given to my Mom at the Municipal Workers Union. The employees there help us out a great deal: they often give me school supplies and sometimes even powdered milk and cans of food.

I don't like going to kindergarten. I cry a lot because I don't want to be there, I want to go to work with my mother in the Munincipal Clinic. I hate the kindergarten, all the teachers and kids alike. Luckily for me, a miracle soon occurs; shortly after enrolling, the director writes in the notebook reserved for communicating with the parents something that I can't quite make out, but seeing as there's a '$' sign, I guess it's about money.

Mum looks at it and says to me, "My dear boy, you'll no longer be going to Pimpollitos."

"Why's that?"

"Well, the director is demanding we pay her for two months in arrears. I simply can't afford it so you'll have to stay home alone for a while."

I'm quite content with this arrangement. I like being poor and unable to attend kindergarten. It means I get to stay at home with my dogs, Lulu and Toti, doing as we please.

I wonder how long this newfound freedom will last me.

What is the true meaning of being free?

CHAPTER THREE
Eva
Obitas et vives

Today I'm very sad, really quite dismayed: returning from a quick forage for firewood, accompanied as always by my faithful dog Lulu, crossing back across the Pan-American Highway, she gets distracted by I'll never know what and a car hits her, throwing her body up into the air and almost breaking it in two. She lands on the roadside, slumped in a heap, and I scream with fright, feeling her pain all at once, not knowing what to do.

My mind is in a state of alarm as I stand over her, equally as paralysed as she is. No car stops to help. There's no one around on foot. And she keeps looking at me with her beautiful black eyes as the blood seeps from all over her body. My eyes fill with tears and my heart with her suffering; I can see she's not yet ready to give in to death.

Lulu is my best friend and she's dying in front of me, but I cannot allow her to remain in agony and in pain, just as my grandmother Raquel suffered, for a full forty-two hours, after she too was hit by a car.

I react; I remember my grandmother and my mother telling me that no animal should be caused unnecessary suffering, but I do not know if they were referring to a situation like this.

Without further reflection, I take a big, thick stick from the pile I've been carrying and, kneeling by her side, planting a sweet farewell kiss on her bloodied little head, I end her life myself. No feelings of remorse, but rather an ocean swell of humanity rolling down my arm.

I then lift her back into my arms, hug her now breathless

body and, feeling her warm blood against my chest, take her back to my shanty. There, with the help of my mum, I dig a hole at the end of our patch and offer her a simple but dignified burial. Lulu is gone now, and with her, much of my daily joy.

I'm looking forward to my first day in school this year. I've dreamed of putting on a new white coat, a white shirt, and wearing a blue tie around my neck. Mum tells me that the President Juan Perón wants the only privileged ones to be us, the children of Argentina, that's why he wants us covered in white. I think it's so poverty and grime can go unnoticed. But I can't imagine that going to school could ever be such a horrible experience. It takes me a long time to work out that I do genuinely hate having to attend school.

I always look forward to seeing my mother Ester waiting for me right outside the school's gates. Before she died, grandma Raquel used to come and collect me but it wasn't the same.

My mum sometimes accompanies me on my walk to school, but, to tell the truth, 'accompany' isn't quite the right word; she drags me by force, her fingers pulling on my ears, grabbing me tightly by the neck, pushing me forward and generally preventing me from running away by any means possible.
Today she lifts me up by the hair to avoid stepping in a puddle. Other parents who are dropping their kids off in the

car look on scandalised, while my tiny body dangles from its hair clasped tightly in her right hand. They honk their horns yelling "murderer!" at my mother. I start to kick and squeal, now truly in the grips of a blustery tantrum. I cry, cry and cry, screaming out "Help! Help!" just like they do in the comics, then lashing out at her with my teeth until she finally prevails in the contest and manages to deliver me to the school grounds.

Once there, the head porter, Sra. Irma, looks down at me with a grave expression that fills me with dread and then says curtly, "Go and form up in the yard". I trudge off to the yard silently obedient.

After another spell of tears, I make it through the school day. As more of them go by, I gradually get used to this new obligation to sit through classes. But every now and then I have a fit and refuse to go. I'm still unhappy with the arrangement.

Then, a few months into my schooling and to my surprise, I find myself selected to be a standard-bearer. I get good marks because, in effect, I attend school twice a day. My mum takes evening lessons to complete her year 4 and since she has no one to leave me with, she brings me along with her. What I learn about there is far more advanced than at my school; Maths and Spanish quickly become my favourite subjects. I listen closely, jotting down everything her teachers say, surrounded by all the adults in the class. I even help mum do her homework when we are at home. My own teachers, meanwhile, are unaware of my double schooling and are rather surprised at what I know. I think that's why they rewarded me with the status of standard-bearer.

At 4.50 every afternoon, the standard-bearer has to form the year groups into lines, ordered from lowest to highest, smallest pupils at the front, tallest at the back. My friend Marcelo Modano and I always compete to be first in line. I think it might just be that we're both quite short. I'd say I'm seven centimetres short of satisfaction, and nine of perfection.

This daily group formation is done in the large 'covered' patio, so called because of its sheet metal roof. Once out there, in order to line up neatly with the right distance between us, we're supposed to stretch our right arm out and rest a hand on the shoulder of the classmate in front. Then we prepare for the lowering of the flag.

Of course, as I'm more often than not first in the line, due to my height, I'm the only one who doesn't have to put my arm out. If I did, I think I'd look like one of those nasty German Nazis from the movies they show on TV at the house of my other Grandmother, Berta.

Anyway, first we all have to sing the flag anthem and then us lucky few, the top students from each year group, acting as sacred standard-bearers, have to lower the national flag and leave it on the headteacher's desk.

But we cannot simply fold the flag any old way. We have to wrap it up like a bun, leaving the emblematic Sun of May beaming up from the middle. It's as hard as it is fun. The headteacher Elena explains to us that the national insignia is not to be folded, washed, patched, or of course burned. Due to these varying restrictions, our flag is only ever wrinkled, dirty and frayed. Since I'm the littlest in school, both in age and stature, the bigger boys always make me carry the flag over to the headmistress' desk. It's a task that I can't say I dislike by any means: it gives me honour to walk past the other students bearing the national insignia in my hands, and an intense feeling of pride which tastes at once sweet and strange.

The teachers and two hundred or so students are well aware that I live in a shanty, because many of them pass by the door of our rickety house twice a day, coming and going from school. I overhear one of my classmates telling another that, "Esteban lives in a pigsty", but I can't say much because I don't know what the word means. I discreetly pluck the dictionary from the teacher's desk and look up the word pigsty under the letter "P". I find it nestled between the words 'poverty' and 'potion' (in Spanish, of course). The definition calls it a "stinking and disgusting place". This makes me very glum: there's poverty in my house, it's true, but it is *not* a stinking or disgusting place.
Now that I understand his insult, I have a good mind to crack my fist on his face, but I hold back swallowing down my bitter saliva, crying a little inside, and feeling a deep pain rise up from my chest to my throat. I can accept being poor in money but I outright refuse to be poor in words. So

I find myself constantly looking up new words in a dictionary to enrich me, sensing that the words I say or write have a soul of their own and knowing them enriches mine.

I think the house where I live out the happiest years of my childhood merits a brief description too. It's a squat box set on a large plot of land, eleven metres by twenty-eight, located in what is today the elegant suburb of Lomas de San Isidro. My house is dwarfed on all sides by spectacular mansions and chalet houses of "well-established families" with swimming pools and green gardens. The land where our shack stands belonged to grandma Raquel.

She was born in Chile, but her ancestors lived in Spain about five hundred years ago. Of course, by now they'll all perhaps be dead. When she first moved to Argentina, she lived on Calle Yapeyú in the suburb of Martínez, in the province of Buenos Aires. At the time Raquel buys the land and erects the precarious little hut, the whole neighbourhood was nothing more than open land where cows roamed freely, grazing the area.

So when my dad leaves my mum, she in turn decides to abandon our home at the time which was in a little town called La Cumbre in the Province of Córdoba, in the upper part of the mountains, where we had been living as a 'normal' family, close to where I was born. Mum then brings me and my brother Daniel to live in this shack in Buenos Aires.

It's right in the middle of the plot, a single large room of about thirty square meters with no internal divisions, a dirt floor, and a roof made up of old corrugated sheets, shiny zinc mingled with black bitumen, which look like pieces of holey cardboard.

When it rains, the drops tap away on the roof sheets in an odd melody. The many holes in the sheets enable another layer of rhythmic dripping in varied tones, further complemented by yet more ringing droplets as they splash into the metal buckets we put on the ground to prevent the inside of the house turning the dirt floor into mud.

The good thing about this is that when the earth is at once wet and hot it releases a delightful petrichor; the leaks, however, are a constant battle in life at this new home.

The walls are made up of long planks of old wood stacked on top of each other and lined on the outside by oil cans with the names "Cocinero" and "Siete Días", opened up, flattened and then nailed firmly to the top section of the walls, while below we use Esso and Shell cans, all collected from the newly built Pan American Highway. They say that this new road will open up a direct route to The United States of America. Mum just explains to me that the oil from Cocinero and Siete Días is for humans to eat, whereas the oil from Esso and Shell is what the cars eat.

Where the roof is strapped down to the walls there are a fair number of gaps that we fill with scrunched up balls of newspaper so the wind can't blow in and freeze us all to death.

On the inside, the walls are lined with yellow Kodak packaging from old boxes of X-ray film that Grandma brings home from the hospital once they've been discarded by the people who X-ray the sick. These too are opened up and nailed to the horizontal boards helping keep out the cold drafts.

But somehow or another, especially in winter, the mischievous wind still manages to creep into the house chilling us to the bone. Grandma says that the Japanese are a great nation because everything they make is of good quality, and that they work hard from the moment they get up, which is always very early, to the moment they go to bed, which is very late. They work with the discipline of soldiers on a divine mission, only stopping to eat a little rice and sleep a short while.

I'm very frightened of storms because I can't help thinking that the roof is going to fly off into the air. When the storm of Santa Rosa comes along with clouds of the seven heavens, which the old folk say form over Peru every year, swelling as they cover many, many kilometres south, which decide to burst right above my house, it's quite scary.

After any such storm, the shack is invariably flooded, turning the floor into a network of islands set in a broad lagoon, which on hot days becomes my swimming pool. There I can wallow about in the brown muddy water having a wonderful time. Such fun!

My house isn't exactly a nice colour: half brown from the

already rusting cans covering the wood, the other half a sad grey. But I can't say the lack of material happiness deprives me of any amusement. The door doesn't have a key because it doesn't have a lock either. It can only be closed from the inside by resting a stick on two hooks either side of the doorframe. Whenever we have to close up the house from the outside, we use a simple chain with no lock, key or anything of the like. Mum says there's no way anyone's going to come in and steal, firstly because heaven protects us, but secondly because there's nothing to steal, so the door is always open.

At night, the moon is the only light we have. There's no electricity, no water, no taps, no bathroom, no kitchen, not even coverings for the floor and walls.

But, little by little, as my mum earns money working in the clinic and cleaning houses, the house will be furnished and modernised. Well, at least that's what she says.

Being without water is the biggest challenge. We have to go to Sra. Telma's house to get it, which means hauling buckets from a block away. Our closest neighbours won't give us any water so the first thing mum does in this "Modernisation Project" is to find a second-hand water pump so we can stop relying on any of them.

We head together to Grand Bourg, a place quite far from where we live. We meet someone there who knows someone else from a nearby shanty town who's going to give us the manual water pump. Mum says the poor are usually the most generous. When we finally find the place we're handed a water pump that weighs like a ton. So mum has to call on several unfortunate victims to give us a hand and together we just about lift it onto the diesel train.

A man comes to make a perforation in the ground at home. He finds the first layer of subsoil water at 18 metres and installs the pump. I anxiously follow every step of the "Water at Home" project knowing that it's going to change our lives in a big way. The pump is green and works like a charm. You have to pump by hand of course and I love it. At first, the pump has the upper hand and I have to push with all my might on the long handle to force it back down, but I soon grasp the technique and grow into a practiced pumper in no time. My mum cries tears of joy as she sees the pump finally installed and thanks God for this blessing. She splashes the first few drops of water on my face and gives me a tender hug.

We're all brimming with delight and I start dancing around in the newly-formed puddles of fresh water. I can't see how I'll ever tire of watching the water come out from the beak of this old green Grand Bourg pump.

Mum declares that now we have both land and water, many of our hardships will be overcome.
Almost immediately she sets about planting courgettes, tomatoes, onions, and other green things that don't tempt me a lot. The courgettes are quick to grow and sprout their

yellow flowers, while the tomatoes take quite a long time; what I like most, however, is sugar-cane and we need to wait three months to be able to harvest them. It's absolutely worth it. There's nothing sweeter for me than peeling, chopping and chewing on them to suck out all their goodness. Mum also buys a rooster and a couple of chickens which lay fresh eggs for us.

Don Oscar, our Paraguayan neighbour, has a lemon tree and we have come to a trade agreement: one fresh egg for one freshly picked lemon. In school, I learn that this is called bartering, which is what the indigenous people did with the Spanish colonisers. The problem is that Don Oscar often asks for two eggs in exchange for a lemon, so I have to remind him that that's not what we agreed, that barter must be fair. I wonder if it was kept fair in the time of the conquistadores.

I'm a little older now, almost seven, and although I never get to have a birthday party I'm quite keen to celebrate my life in the hope there may be a present or two for me.

Along comes my birthday and, as promised, my father, with a gift for me. He turns up in the afternoon to hand me a beautiful electric train set: one locomotive with five wagons in trail, some for passengers, and some for cargo. And it comes with ten sections of track that, once assembled, take the shape of a large oval. It's a splendid present, and so unexpected, the only problem being that I don't know where to plug it in. We still don't have electricity at home. I somehow don't think it's going to work with a candle or a kerosene lamp either. Mum says that she might ask a certain Don Justo to install the electricity at home and gradually pay for it in something called 'instalments'.

My glee turns swiftly to glumness. But I assemble my train and its tracks regardless and decide I'll make it run on draught power, that is, move it along with my fingers while at the same time making noises to mimic the train engine. I end up spending hours lying on the ground playing with this electric train without electricity.

After a while, mum asks Don Justo to come over. He's a thin man of about seventy with a kind old face, who always knows how to make me laugh; the neighbours call him *gallego*, meaning 'Galician', but it doesn't seem all that fair to call Don Justo *gallego* because he's actually Andalusian. He himself explains to me that all Spaniards in Argentina get called Galician because most of the Spanish immigrants here hail from Galicia.

Don Justo is extremely gifted with his hands and he installs our electricity without tubing or anything sophisticated, nothing but bare wiring, held up by bent nails fixed to the straps of the shack. And so we now have another good reason to celebrate.

Electric light! I'm beaming. I turn it on, off, on, off, continuously, incredulously. The new lamp feels like another miracle which I'll never tire of fixating upon. I cheer a goodbye to the kerosene lamp and the candles. Mum gives thanks to God for our new light and watches me glowing with joy as I marvel at my new train racing around the track all on its own.

I'm very fond of Don Justo. He's always so friendly to me but he does speak in a funny accent punctuated with lots of 'th' sounds. He also strangely addresses me using the polite term '*usted*', a formality reserved for adults, apparently ignoring that I'm only a small child.

He sometimes gets very worked up telling his stories, his voice and expression revealing some deep-rooted pain. I can't gather much about it but he tells us that he was in the Sahara Desert and speaks of a war in Spain that lasted three sad years in which brothers killed brothers. A war in which he fought and lost. That's why he left his country. After being imprisoned and tortured with a long stick, receiving electric shocks. He dreamt of coming to the Republic of Argentina to live in peace. He says that back in his home country there's now a dictator who keeps everyone in check, that he feels much better off in Argentina, though there are sometimes generals in power here too, that he can't return to his old country because *Generalísimo* Franco, who's no ordinary general, isn't too keen on freedom nor does he want my friend Don Justo returning to Spain any time soon.

The kitchen is actually the same room we sleep in and consists of nothing more than a hole in the ground which we stock with firewood or charcoal. I love putting dry eucalyptus branches on the fire and listening to them pop and crackle as they burn, releasing a citrus aroma that spreads throughout the house.

Our main cooking utensil is a large old can, once filled with sweet potatoes jam. Sitting on a stack of bricks, I busy myself happily stirring away in some potpourri or other as mum sits next to me supervising. "I can't teach you to cook, Esteban, only to stir. I don't know how to cook." She goes on to say I'm practically a gourmet Argentine chef already. After finishing dinner, we have to stay awake a while waiting for the embers to fade out or douse the hearth with water. Mum says that if we don't, we may end up dying in our sleep in the middle of the night. It sounds kind of fun to die like this, completely unaware, but then I wonder if we all die in our sleep, who will bury us? I quickly come to the conclusion it's better not to die at all.

Of all the faults our house has, the most problematic is the bathroom. We don't really have one anymore. I mean, there is one, but it's become quite a dangerous affair to use it: the pit is almost full and the wooden boards covering it are old and rotting, so every time you squat to take aim, there's a grave risk you'll fall in. Mum is on the case again, but everything takes time. It turns out having a new bathroom built isn't cheap either.

First, she needs to find someone with muscles strong enough to dig a big new hole in the ground, and then have them build the latrine on top of it.

Mum won't let me use the word *shit*, she wants me to say 'faecal matter' or 'faeces' instead. She says it sounds better, I'm less convinced: it's just as disgusting whether you give it a nice name or not.

Petty disputes aside, my very enterprising mother, with the aspirations of an architect, takes it upon herself to build a temporary bathroom herself. To do so, she plants three large metal sheets about ten centimetres into the ground, standing up to form like three sides of a square. It's set at the back of the plot, about seven metres from the shack. Mum puts a curtain on the empty side to act as a door, not bothering with the roof or window, and it's job done! With so many holes in the sheet metal, I can't imagine a roof and window are entirely necessary.

We now have to call it the 'toilet'. Mum insists on us using weird words for these things so I obey her without a fuss. We *defecate* on some old newspaper, then wrap it up and throw it into the rubbish bin. I often play a little game: I look through the papers for pictures of the villainous moustachioed military men and aim for their faces!

Winters and summers are equally tough at home. We have two large legless beds, their metal springs peeking through holes, their frames upheld by more stacked bricks; there's no jumping on the beds otherwise everything would fall apart and we'd land hard onto the dirt floor. In one bed sleep my mother and I, in the other is my uncle Marcelo. I love my uncle very dearly, not only because he's an orphan now but because he's always taking care of me and

36

giving me cups of black tea and a piece of bread. The bread is quite hard so he shows me the best way to eat it by dipping it in the tea. Yum!

Mum is left with the upkeep of the house on her own. But she now has another son: her brother Marcelo is only a few years older than me, so he feels like more of a brother to me than an uncle.

My real older brother Daniel, who's also a few years older than me and has been living with my paternal grandparents all this time, loves our dad so much but feels distraught and betrayed when he's sent away to an English boarding school in Hurlingham, a suburb which is far away and has a name I never know how to pronounce. My father says he's only doing it to rescue him from the awful life my mother has in store for him. Luckily he decides to leave me at home with my mother, perhaps because I'm too young. What a relief!

One day I come home to find we have a new piece of furniture: a plain rectangular table. Only underneath it, there's a large seal that looks like it was stamped with something hot, just like the marks you see on cows. I think this seal is the first thing I ever read on my own, without anyone's help. The label says, "Eva Perón Foundation".

As it happens, I end up spending a fair amount of time on the dirt floor under that table, most of it trying to catch mice in a jar with a bait of bread. I wait around for hours for some hungry little fellow to come and try his luck. The mice are simply too quick for me, however, so hunting them proves no easy task.

For all my guile and patience I succeed just once in my attempts as a trapper. But to my horror, the prize is a tiny one indeed, much too unseasoned to be worthy of pride on my part. I feel sorry watching it struggle so helplessly and think of its parents and siblings who'll no doubt be worried sick searching for it. My desire for vengeance subsides, I cannot ignore my pity for the creature any longer so I resolve to release it asking only that it not return to our shack to steal more bread. There's hardly enough food to go around as it is!

One thing is for sure, we aren't alone in the house. No, we have to share this shelter with a whole host of cockroaches, mice and ants. We therefore have to safely seal all our food in big glass jars to keep out all the pesky scroungers.

During my early years at school it's General Alejandro Agustín Lanusse's turn to be the de facto president of the country. He lives next to the Cabildo, the oldest building in Buenos Aires still standing from the time of Spanish rule; that's the building I find myself drawing one day on a piece of cardboard at school. In the absence of glue, I have to make a light paste of water and flour and stick glitter to the Cabildo in the national colours of white and sky blue.

Juan, now one of my best new friends, is the grandson of General Lanusse. He lives in a big house near my shack, on Calle Jacinto Díaz, just around the corner from Pimpollitos, my old kindergarten. We met at Lolita's grocery store. One morning he comes into the shop with his mother and I ask him if he knows how to suck chocolate milk through his nose. He says he doesn't, and I reply that I don't either. Juan bursts out laughing at this and almost immediately invites me to his birthday party. So Lolita takes care of bathing me and dressing me up while my mum Ester wraps up a blue cuddly rabbit for me to give to Juan as his seventh birthday present, it was given to her by an admirer. Personally, I find it a rather silly present to give him. Rabbits aren't usually known for being blue, are they?

Off I go to Juan's house for the first time, as the only guest from the neighbourhood, and there I meet his family. His dad is Roberto Rimoldi Fraga, another important person so I'm told. Who knows why but they say he's very respectable.

I spend much of my time at the party eating and drinking my way through as much as possible, while at the same time trying to do so as delicately as Mirtha would. Juan sweetly tells me that my blue rabbit is his favourite present of the day.
His parents stare and point at me while talking to other adults, a few of them even come and ask me my name, ruffling my hair, which makes me very angry. I don't want them ruining my hairstyle. I hate it when grown-ups touch my head.

Afterwards, when I get home, my mum and a few other curious neighbours bombard me with questions about the Lanusse family. They ask me about the other guests; they all want to know if the President of the Republic was there.

I explain that I wasn't particularly attentive to who was around me because I was too busy practicing the good manners I'd learnt on TV from Mirtha Legrand.

Juan quickly becomes my best friend. I think I'm his best friend too. He's always saying that his grandfather's in Buenos Aires, instead of just calling it *Capital Federal* which is what we say, so I ask him one time, "Where do you think you are now, silly, the Belgian Congo?" Lolita later explains to me that for well-to-do people the Federal Capital is simply known as Buenos Aires.

Sadly, Juan's family doesn't stay for long in Las Lomas de San Isidro. After a year of friendship, his grandpa has a moment of 'divine enlightenment' and calls for the re-organisation of political parties, whatever that means. Anyhow, following the new elections, Lanusse leaves the Casa Rosada, the pink presidential residence, and his grandchildren shortly afterwards leave our neighbourhood too.

Juan Perón returns from Spain to govern Argentina once again. There's quite a lot of fuss about it at home and even more when he dies soon after taking office, leaving his third wife Isabelita as president. A couple of years later, she too would be overthrown and the military would be back in power for another eight long years of gloom in the Casa Rosada. You see, apparently the military has this nasty habit of kicking out the government every now and again and appointing themselves heads of the state.

I don't know who Eva Perón is, but Mum and grandma Raquel are always chatting about her, so is Don Justo. I imagine her as something of a sacred and beautiful virgin who works miracles, distributes toys to the all the nation's children and somehow even sends tables to their shanties. All this, even though she's supposedly dead.

Grandma Berta doesn't like Evita one bit; grandma Raquel on the other hand showers her with praise at every opportunity. For starters, she shares her surname with the Perón family. Mum explains to me that she was the second wife of General Perón and that although she's been dead for many years now, Evita is still alive and well in the hearts of millions of Argentines. She goes on to say that Evita died very young, when she was only thirty-three years old, but that before leaving the world, she had said, "I will return and I will be millions". I don't quite understand but I think it's something to do with religion.

I can picture Evita returning, resurrected from the dead, though the part about her being 'millions' doesn't quite find expression in my large, but in this case limited, imagination.

The story gets even better when mum tells me of how, when Evita died, they embalmed her body… her fair white skin, her beautiful blonde hair, her perfectly sculpted shape… and kept it in the union headquarters of the General Confederation of Labour for a year. I'm listening in raptures until suddenly, my eyes are struck open in disbelief, no doubt left looking like a pair of fried eggs, as I learn that this nice body is then stolen away by the military, put on a plane and flown to Brussels, the capital of Belgium, incidentally, home of chocolate and the Manneken Pis; from there, it is taken to Bonn, the capital of the Federal Republic of Germany; and then put on a train to Roma, which is 'love' spelt backwards in Spanish, and the capital of Italy and good pizza; until finally, it came to rest in Milan, the capital of fashion, where it was buried under the false name of Maria Maggi in a Milanese cemetery, which brings to my mind a *milanesa*, a sort of schnitzel we sometimes eat at home, but I think in this case it has more to do with the Italian city.

I listen to this overload of information with wondrous surprise, and a little fright too. Mum soon continues the tale explaining that after several years Evita's body was unearthed and on the move again, traveling through France, the country of revolutions, to Madrid, the capital of the Motherland and good sun. There, Juan Perón kept the body of his second wife in his house for a number of years, the very house he was at the time sharing with his third wife, Isabelita. At this point in the story, my mind now overflowing with all sorts of colours and images, I begin to picture the bigamous General Perón living with his two wives under the same roof and remember my unfaithful father keeping a mistress, the blonde Betty of La Falda, at the same time as he was living with my mother.

I find it strangely comforting that Perón didn't deceive Isabelita in the same way my father cheated on my mum, for one wife was alive and the other dead. I am nevertheless soon unsettled again when mum adds that Juan Perón declared Evita was not in fact dead, only sleeping. I just can't see how anyone could sleep through such a commotion!

To round off her novel story, mum says that on the orders of Isabelita, who's now President of the Republic, Evita's body has been returned to Buenos Aires to rest at last in the Duarte family pantheon in the cemetery of Recoleta in Buenos Aires, the capital of Argentina and the tango.

One day, not too far off, I think about how wonderful it would be if I could travel in life to even half the cities Evita did in death.

Anyhow, now we have electricity at home, mum's colleagues at the Union gave us an old TV. It's definitely seen better days but I'm just thrilled it turns on.

I used to sit in front of it all day watching the black-and-white figure of Juan Perón. He is after all the husband of the holy virgin who gave us that table. I love it when he gives a speech live on national television. It means I can flick through all five of the channels, and there he is on every one of them. I like that he speaks without reading much from his notes. I don't understand anything he actually says but I like his voice, it sounds kind and he has a broad smile with bright white teeth.

I learn a song about him and start singing it happily and often. But a few years later mum forbids me to do so anymore because the military have moved back into the Casa Rosada and she says they take as their prisoners anyone caught singing Perón's song.

I'm not too happy about this new rule though so, as often as I care to, I run off far from my mother's ears to the bridge over Blanco Encalada, where the Panamerican Highway hums away loudly above me, and there I sing out to the unspeakable old man, "Perón, Perón, how great you are, my General, how valuable you are…" Oh, it gives me such a kick! As my simple little melody echoes out under the bridge, I feel this ridiculous surge of Peronist passion, perhaps triggered by the allure of the forbidden.

The military end up banning all songs about Perón, even mentioning his name is a crime. They also ban all movies with rude words, naked people, and stories about men leaving their wives for other women and vice versa. Even 'The Little Prince', one of the books we have at home, is forbidden as well. Mum says it's considered *subversive*, whatever that means.

I have to go and hide myself in a trunk every time I want to read it, so no one can accuse me of being a little revolutionary or anarchist. It's all very confusing.

Anyway, one cold and wet winter day, Perón gets a call from heaven and that's that. Kaput.

Mum starts crying uncontrollably. Me too, but I can't tell whether I'm crying for Perón or just from seeing my mum in a state. She blubbers that life is short and unpredictable, that it's a gift not an acquired right, and that we must all live prepared to die as Perón was. I only pick up half the things she says, but I don't bother her for more because I can see how very upset she is.

I watch the whole funeral on TV, scarcely looking away for a second. So many people line up to see his embalmed body, thousands and thousands of Peronists and other curious people all queued up outside a place called Capilla Ardiente, 'Burning Chapel', but it's not actually burning.

I begin to wonder what an embalmed body smells like. The program doesn't offer any clues but I keep my eyes glued to the screen anyway. I just want to see if I can spot my neighbour Don Totu in the crowd somewhere. He's there at the funeral with his daughter Ariadna who's my classmate.

Perón dies just like grandma Raquel did, but their surname lives on with Isabelita, even though she's actually called María Estela Martínez Cartas. She was already the vice president of the Republic but now she's becoming the first female president in Argentine history. I quite like her too. I think she looks so nice dressed in a plaid suit, her hair pulled up in a bun like a ballet dancer. But she normally wears a black gown, Zorro-style, and her accent is a strange mix of Riojan (Argentina) and Castilian.

When she gives her speeches on TV, her voice is almost screaming and often she can't hold back her tears. When the military force her out of the Casa Rosada, just like they did with Arturo Umberto Illia Francesconi, she leaves in a helicopter, in one of those she has flown once visiting the Boulogne military factory which is near my house. After she's sent to prison for a while, she then goes to live in Madrid at Calle Moreto, 3. It's called *exile*.

The Perón couple adored Spain; indeed, the General was, right up to his death, a friend of the Generalísimo, about whom Don Justo had spoken with such pain and hatred. Franco welcomed them to the 'motherland' with open arms at a place called La Puerta de Hierro, "The Iron Gate". What a fitting name for it! The Argentinian military would never be able to capture or kill them once they went through it.

Spain becomes quite a special place for me too, even though I've never set foot there. It's just that lots of my friends are so-called *Galicians*. Some are like Don Justo and others live in the big beautiful houses around us. I'm particularly fond of Carlitos and Antonia. Both of them talk using that same 'th' sound, which I can now imitate quite well, my schoolmates find it very funny.
I'm so fascinated with the country, I learn to draw the map of it with my eyes closed, including the layout of its main rivers: the Ebro, the Guadalquivir and the Tajo. I also tell lots of Galician jokes to my friends, without malice, of course. At school we're taught to love and respect this

Motherland, we're told it gave birth to all Argentines.

Mum says that Spain has a very large moral debt to Argentina, and Mexico for that matter. During the civil war in which Don Justo fought and lost, and even before that, she tells me that many Spaniards were kept alive thanks to the grain and meat that our two countries sent them. On top of that, we always kept our doors open for Spanish exiles, like Don Justo, who left in search of freedom and a better life.

I wonder if Spain will ever pay this debt she's talking about. After such a long time should debts be forgiven?

CHAPTER FOUR
Mirtha
Educator and chic

Today I skipped school, or as the grown-ups say, "played truant". I do it quite often actually, just to stay at home watching the television, which has a croaky sound and a fuzzy image that looks like it's raining. One of my favourite shows is "Lunch with Mirtha Legrand". It starts at 1pm, exactly when I have my afternoon classes. Mum is away at work, of course. Some people there say she took up the position left by my grandma. Some evil tongues even say it was nepotism but I'm not persuaded, especially seeing as I don't understand what that word means.

When mum returns from work around 3pm in the afternoon, Mirtha's TV live lunches are already over and I'm hiding away in an old, ramshackle, rusty trunk behind the house. I lie there thinking, reading or napping until ten past five or so, and then I magically appear as if having just come home from school. The problem is that I don't have a watch; in fact, watches and clocks are quite conspicuous for their absence in our home. Grandma Raquel and mum both seem to wake up by some form of mind control. But Grandma's not here anymore. I guess that must make it harder. I can't get used to the fact Grandma's gone, I talk about her like she's still alive sometimes. It's true we are aided somewhat by our crowing cockerels. I can imitate them perfectly now and occasionally enjoy setting them off myself with a long squawking laugh, which they quickly follow up like a philharmonic cackling choir. It makes me see myself as their conductor.

In the afternoons, I can always tell when five o'clock comes around as I hear the uproar from all the kids leaving school.

As they pass by my door, I step out from my secret hiding place as casually as possible.

I simply can't help myself, I just love sitting down to lunches with Mirtha Legrand. And it's on five times a week… I'm not only drawn in by the rich delicacies from across the lands which are served up for Mirtha and her guests, things I've never seen or heard of, which she always says at the end are all totally delicious, but while she herself is obviously cultured and intelligent, she manages to come across as such a kind person on TV. No one seems to know her age, but she always looks young and fresh-faced.

Sadly, there's no playing truant on Tuesdays because mum has the day off and if she knew I was skiving off to see 'La Chiqui' Legrand, she'd most certainly fly into one of her crazy fits of rage and give me a good beating. Honestly, I think she sometimes takes pleasure from hitting me with a broom.

I don't really like how lady Legrand is called 'La Chiqui', because she's not actually *chiquita* (tiny), she's great. But she herself explains that Chiqui was a nickname given to differentiate her from her beloved twin sister 'Goldy' who is a few minutes older than her. Mirtha's guests at these fancy lunches are usually well known characters from public life, though she does sometimes invite normal nobodies and poor people too.

One day she eats with Carlos Monzón, a quick and violent boxer who's also the boyfriend of another TV star I really like called Susana Giménez. Susana's a blonde actress, with very striking looks and a friendly manner who I've often seen in TV adverts. She's very quiet and I can't imagine her ever getting angry, not to mention smashing an ashtray over someone's head. These days she's featured in a provincial lottery advert called *Cha, Cha, Chaqueña*. Another day, I find Mirtha at her table with a comedian called Pepito Marrone who often starts his sentences letting out a long "cheeeee", moving his lips to the left. Also sitting at the table is a twelve-year-old boy. He shows off some pictures he once took of UFOs flying over Buenos Aires. I wish I had a camera to catch UFOs on film; that way Mirtha might invite me to be on her show and eat at her table too.

I can see from her expression that Mirtha isn't convinced about the existence of UFOs, but she says nothing. Perhaps she doesn't want to embarrass the poor boy. I know I believe in them: my ego isn't big enough to think we're alone in the universe.

I can tell from watching her that Mirtha has a very strong character, though she usually knows how to control herself. She sometimes lays into the people who work on the show, regardless of whether it's live or not. She turns in annoyance asking, "What's the matter back there, guys? Why are you chatting? Is there something funny? Something wrong? No? It's just quite distracting… keep quiet please…"
She's always complaining about all the taxes she has to pay on her salary.

Seeing how much she and her guests eat, it's as if I'm there having lunch with them too, and I start to feel quite full. Watching these shows all the time, I can imagine how they help feed millions of poor Argentines who are surely just as hungry as I am.

Today, as on every 29th of the month, they eat gnocchi, first sliding some money under the plate. I'd love to try gnocchi sometime, even if it's without the money under my plate for good luck.

Mirtha announces that she's been in the Soviet Union, presenting a film she made with her husband Daniel Tinayre. She says she had to give a speech in Russian and then repeats it all by heart leaving me stunned. I think I'd like to learn a few languages like Mirtha. She speaks French very well and Spanish even better, though she does sometimes invent words. Today she described someone as "*aganico*", that is, someone without the '*ganas*' or will to do anything. I'm amazed when I find out that this doesn't exist in the Spanish dictionary.

I also learn from her how to behave at a formal lunch: not rest my elbows on the table, wipe my mouth with the napkin before drinking, and not talk with my mouth full. I suppose I have to forgive her for her constant interruptions. Though I can't say I care too much because thanks to her I've learnt good table manners.

It wouldn't be too much to say that I've really come to idolise Sra. Legrand: she's sublime and sweet, cute and elegant, all of which mean pretty much the same but it's no less true.

She seems to have a lot of money too, and yet she's always saying the dresses she wears are lent to her. At the start of each show she appears with a new look, unfailingly repeats her catchphrase, which I like saying along with her, with a certain flamboyance, *"En la mesa hoy tenemos rosas rococó rosadas"* (Today on the table we have pink Rococo roses), and then gives a little spin. As televisions are still black and white, she spends a lot of time just explaining what colour everything is: her clothes, her shoes, the flowers, the food…

I can see Mirtha is very patriotic too, and she continually reminds us that the most important thing in life is family. She's well-spoken and never says rude words on TV; I'm pretty sure she doesn't in her private life either. I bet she'd turn red like a tomato if she heard someone say 'shit' or the f-word. It's as if she thinks swearing would somehow sully her lips.

I really like television, you know, but I don't get how it works. Sometimes my mind wanders and I picture the actors taking some magic potion so they can shrink down and walk into the TV through the antenna and cables. I also imagine that just as we can see and listen to those on TV, they too can also hear and see us at the other end.

One day I'm watching the news on channel thirteen where I see the presenter Roberto Maidana looking right at me as I squat over a chamber pot in front of the TV. I suddenly get

54

very embarrassed and start to worry if, in addition to seeing me, he can smell too. It sounds crazy I know, but one day it could happen. Or not?

The news is always fascinating. I don't know what's going on most of the time, but I like the voices of the presenters, especially that of Sergio Villaruel, who in spite of his moustache actually speaks really well, with a lovely turn of phrase.

My favourite shows are "The Adventures of Zorro", a cartoon called "Hijitus", "The Three Stooges", a soap about a primary-school teacher called "Jacinta Pichimahuida", "Batman", "The Lone Ranger", "Lassie", a cooking show with "Doña Petrona", a comedy show called "La Tuerca", and anything with Tato Bores in it. On top of that, there are a few other soap operas I try not to miss if I can help it: an Argentinian one called "Malevo" and two Mexican ones called "Italian girl comes to get married" and "I buy that woman". In my opinion, none even come close to "Lunch with Mirtha Legrand", I would never want to miss it for the world, but I do have to go to school sometimes.

The grocery shop run by Lolita and her husband Don Ponce is only a few metres from my house. It's like a mini supermarket where they sell everything: fresh bread, fruit and veg, cleaning products, cured meats, bottled milk—and also milk from "Las Tres Niñas" that now comes in a strange carton shaped like a triangle—plain yogurt in glass jars made by "la Vascongada", all sorts of sweets, like "Topolin" lollipops which come with surprises or little

"Jack" chocolates with figurines inside, and a whole load of drinks and other tasty stuff.

Lolita is so very sweet to me and I love her as if she's another Grandmother. They have five dogs in total, of which Toti and Pamela are my favourites. There's hardly a hair on their bodies, just a few tufts on their heads and legs. They tell me Toti is a Xoloitzcuintle, which is also thankfully known as an Aztec dog (slightly easier to pronounce!), since it comes from Mexico, while Pamela is a Chinese Crested dog. But Lolita adds that the dogs are in fact "Tucumanos" because she brought them from Tucumán, the smallest and greenest province in Argentina. She has to keep a close eye on them at all times in case they decide to run off. If they're caught and taken to the municipal dog pound, they'll be gassed to death, like any dog found wandering the streets of San Isidro with no owner.

Behind the shop is the house, and behind the house is a small garden where Don Ponce breeds frogs. He has them in a huge container of water in the shade of a yellow plum tree whose branches hang down heavy-laden with fruit. Don Ponce says he has more frogs than all his fingers and toes added up together.
He tells me he keeps the frogs to eat them but I don't fall for it because every time I'm around there they're never any fewer. He must be about sixty years old and he's constantly doing these things Lolita calls 'naughty pranks'. I love playing pranks too. I notice they make my heart beat much

faster and I enjoy the excitement.

One evening at sunset, Don Ponce climbs up onto the roof of the store with a crate of smelly rotten peaches and starts lobbing them over at our house. When they hit the metal roof they make a loud thud and smash to pieces. He seems to be enjoying himself quite a lot. Meanwhile, I'm shaking in fear and mum doesn't know whether to go and complain or not. She still owes Lolita and Don Ponce money from our tab but has no money to settle up yet. We always buy from them "*al fiado*", which means on *faith* or credit, very different to paying with cash. Mum explains to me that the trade works because there's *faith* that the debt will be repaid. If it is indeed repaid, mum calls that *good faith*, which she says is the foundation of the world and impossible to live without. I'm not sure if that relation between words is true or not but it all makes good sense to me.

We go to the grocery store, we ask Lolita to fetch us what we need, she writes it down in two notebooks, one for her and one for us, and at the end of the month when mum receives her salary (I like this word a lot because it sounds a bit like salt and means we can trade it for fruit and maybe some chocolate too), they both do their sums in their booklets—no calculators, no talking, just using their heads, just musing the numbers quickly across their lips—and finally when they agree on the total debt to be paid, mum gives the money to Lolita.

Lolita often gives us a discount, which means she charges a

little less. Lolita's mum is from Switzerland and comes to visit her once a year. She doesn't speak any Spanish but we still manage to understand each other quite well. She's very old and elegant, only ever dressed in black, and I often see her sitting under a grapevine of Muscat writing out long letters in German. One time she offers me a handful of Swiss chocolates. The mere sight of them gives me the sensation they're already melting in my mouth. I stare at her full of tenderness, unable to hold back my tears. She too reminds me of my grandma Raquel.

Mum usually won't let me pick up anything but bread and milk from the grocery store.
When one Christmas comes along, feeling that it's some sort of a party, I pluck up the courage to get a sweet bread called Panettone that Mirtha Legrand was talking about on TV. I go and buy it on *faith*, take it home and, with all the love I can muster, hand it to mum as a Christmas present. She flies into another of her fits and screams at me that we don't eat Panttone that it's for other people, that we don't celebrate Christmas or Christmas Eve at home, and that I should immediately go and return it to the store. Shocked and ashamed, I trundle off back to Lolita and explain to her that we can't eat the Panettone because we don't celebrate Christmas *or* Christmas Eve. Lolita listens carefully to my story, smiles at me with a look of pity and crosses the sweet bread off from both notebooks, hers and ours. I return home glumly and head straight to the chicken coop where our laying hen, Zulema, is and I steal an egg from her instead. I decide that I can ease my sorrow beating the yolk

up with some sugar but I fear that Zulema could report me to the police.

Grown-ups say that these are difficult times for Argentina. But I'm told that our country's name comes from the word *argentum*, from Latin, a language whose origins puzzle me, which means silver (a bit like *argenterie* in French, the language of France). The man who invented Argentina only called it that because when he arrived from Spain he thought the colour of the sea-like river looked silver. So, at that moment, he took it to mean there was lots of silver here. That's why it's called Rio de la Plata today. But the grown-ups say the military and some of the politicians stole all the money, so I think we have to change the name of our country, call it something like the 'Republic of Tin', to show that it's not worth as much.

Mum says the military has a nasty habit of overthrowing our democratically elected civilian government. All those grown-up words are a bit much for me, but I get the sense that the military does things it shouldn't.

She says that first they 'usurped' (another strange word) the authority of Dr. Arturo Illia—a man who loves Córdoba as much as I do, who was also a good, tender and honest grandfather—kicking him out of the Casa Rosada, where the rulers live and work, and so the custom of usurping governments goes on.

I wonder if this unfortunate habit of the military will ever end. Or that taking power by force is part of the military's nature?

CHAPTER FIVE
Lolita
Employer and benefactor

It's a few days until my birthday. For the first time in my life I'm going to celebrate it with a party. I'm as delighted as I am anxious. Lolita, who's now my boss, is organising the celebration in her house with cake and all sorts of treats. She says that the mood in my house is a little too sad, it lacks the colour and space fit for a birthday party; her house, on the other hand, is ideal with its big living room, long table, armchairs, and even windows with curtains.
Tomorrow, straight after school, six of my best friends are coming over. Never have I thought Lolita more wonderful than now. What's more, I get the feeling that she only gave me work in the store because of how much she loves me.

It's been almost a year since I started working at *Lolita's*, going in every morning at 8 a.m., stocking the fridges, keeping everything clean, sweeping the floor, getting the fruit and veg in order, wrapping up the eggs by the half-dozen in old newspaper, nice and slow so the eggs don't break; then, after a quick sandwich, I'm off to school for 12:45 p.m.

Of course, on many occasions, I only pretend to go as it's much more fun staying home to watch Mirtha's lunches. On other days I genuinely do want to attend lessons but the school is closed for "disinfecting" (I have a feeling the staff just don't want to come in, in the same way I sometimes don't) or because there's a mad rapist on the loose. That's when I have to be extra careful walking about the streets. I scan the treetops around me just to make sure he's not about to pounce on me from above.

Last year I hit a record of low attendance in school. I skipped a total of sixty days, plus there was a teacher's strike that lasted almost a month. Pure bliss!

Today is my special day. We're on a long break that usually lasts fifteen minutes but, to the joyful surprise of all, is turning into nearly an hour. Soon I notice the teachers have a scrambled look on their faces. Seeing as the bells still haven't rung, something I usually obsess over, I want to find out what's going on. I see Srta. Neta, who's in charge of year seven, now with quite a grave expression, surrounded by several other teachers, one of whom is Srta. Naomi Catalani de Bellini, the acting headteacher who replaced the witch Srta. Polsson, all of them silent. They're listening carefully, now with occasional gasps, to the instructions coming from a transistor radio held by Srta. Bellini. Shortly afterwards, the teachers order us back to the classrooms to gather all our belongings, then head to the courtyard to form up in lines and wait for the headteacher to address us all. Today it's my turn to lower the national flag. Srta. Neta approaches me solemnly and tells me very earnestly to lower the flag completely this time, but without unhooking it, because we are going to fix a black ribbon to it and then raise it again, just to half-mast.
"Do you understand?" She asks me.
"No, ma'am, I don't, because I don't know what half-mast is. Please can you explain it?"
She says that after we put the black ribbon on the flag, I have to raise it once more, but only halfway up the pole. She adds that today we're not going to be singing the flag

anthem because today is now a day of mourning. Of course I don't know what mourning means either, but this time I say nothing. I imagine it's something to do with pain and instinctively gag a little.

Srta. Bellini explains that today is a very sad day because Generalissimo Francisco Franco has just died and President Isabelita, that same president I really like, has decreed a week of national mourning. Srta. Neta then calls for a minute of silence, requesting that each of us should look down at our own feet. It's as if everyone's dismayed, but it's my birthday! I'm not sure what to feel as I stand there. When it's over, we all slowly return to our respective houses very early that day.

I feel like this man has died just to ruin my first birthday party. Anger burns inside me and I want to explode but I hold back. I just can't get my head round why we're meant to be so sad all because far away in Spain the Generalissimo Don Francisco Franco, the same man Don Justo hates with all his heart (I don't care if Isabelita likes him), is dead. He's ruined my first birthday party. What a miserable old killjoy, I tell myself, silently seething, swallowing down the hatred I feel for him, even if he was the ruler of our beloved Motherland… His death has ended the celebration of another year in my life.

Sometimes I think all these bad things happen to me because I'm cursed, like the people in fairytales. I wonder if sleeping with my mouth open allows evil demons to crawl inside me!

I'm one of the few students whose house is well known to all the teachers, for the same reason the students know me: because my rickety shack is only a hundred yards from the school. Srta. Ofelia says that I'm her favourite and I think a few other teachers feel the same way. I don't know why Ofelia calls us *"palomitas blancas"* (little white doves), or why grown-ups are so weird in general. They seem to come out with a lot of rubbish and yet never explain themselves. I feel like they think we boys understand everything when it's often not the case.

I think I get a little too much attention from the teachers. If anyone's starving at school, it's Esteban. If anyone has nits, you can be sure it's Esteban. If anyone has to be exempted from the co-operative payment scheme, it's Esteban. If anyone needs clothes or shoes, it's Esteban. Always Esteban, always me. I'm seen as a rich example for almost everything.

Every week the teachers sell raffle tickets to the students, staff, parents, and anyone else who wants to draw a number for the chance to win a big cake. Then, on Fridays, before we all go home, everyone lines up excitedly in the yard again. The tickets that have been sold are put into a bag and Srta. Elena Manacero, the teacher from 5B, who has the deepest voice of any woman I've ever met—perhaps due to the dozens of cigarettes she smokes every day, both in and out of the classroom—asks us all to be quiet and begins the draw.

Srta. Elena usually calls on the help of Srta. Ofelia, from Year 4, to pick out the lucky number of the winning ticket and hand it to her to be read out, a task that she performs with great art and suspense. In the time I've been at school, I must've won the raffle almost a dozen times. Always Esteban, they say… It seems I'm the luckiest student after all.

Whenever I win I swell with the applause as I step forward to receive the cake as if it were a trophy and off I trot homewards, my mouth already watering behind a greedy grin. I appreciate every little bit of it: the cream, the *dulce de leche*, the sprinkles of coconut and chocolate! But that's not to say I don't share every cake with my mum, my uncle Marcelo, and the dogs and chickens too.

Today I'm popping round to visit Srta. Manacero at her house with two schoolmates because she recently retired. She's a wonderful teacher and an extremely honest person, so honest that she let slip a very well-kept secret. "Esteban," she turns to me innocently, "do you know that Srta. Ofelia often hides your raffle ticket up her sleeve so that you win the cake?" I don't think she's expecting an answer from me, at least I hope not. She goes on, "You see, the teachers believe the cake is more important to you than to many of the other students." I can feel myself blushing now and unable to speak, even if I wanted to. The surprise, anger and shame all at once close up my throat in a big lump. It turns out I'm not the lucky guy I thought I was.

On another day, while being grounded at school, I overhear a conversation among a few teachers in the staff room about the "Rodrigazo" and how all my family and I have at home is hard old bread, already green with mould, and tea without sugar. It's just there's nothing else. I find out Rodrigo is the Minister of Economy in Isabelita's government and he's also known as *Celeste* or something.
I don't know what's exactly wrong with this man, but it turns out he's in a bit of a muddle over the country's maths; he's spent all the money and left much of the country without food. I think it must be the first time in Argentina that both the poor and the rich are having similar difficulties in putting food on the table, the former because they don't have any money to buy food, while the latter have the money but can't find the food: "everything is scarce".

During the fifteen-minute break, the teachers who're on duty are supposed to ruffle through the heads of their "little white doves" as part of a rather intrusive search for lice. As you have guessed, I tend to be their main target. When my head's in their grasp, they always say they're going to throw a little "Lice Party". They confess to me they actually quite enjoy ridding me of lice. Apparently I have a nice head, firstly because my hair is straight, long and blonde, but also because they usually find a good amount of lice in it, enough to occupy both teachers on duty supervising the break anyway. They even find it mildly therapeutic as they feel a short release of tension when squeezing the lice between their fingernails until they burst.

They love the faint "popping" they make as their sides split squirting out a bit of my blood. The eggs, however, stay well stuck to my hair. They say they won't touch them because they're not as fun to pop. What they want to see is blood.

With the other children, the teachers simply say, "You've got lice, so tell your mother to rub Detebencil in your hair". I, on the other hand, receive the full treatment there and then, with four hundred eyes looking at me full of surprise and curiosity. Still, Detebencil smells like kerosene anyway.

But I think these teachers are being a bit cruel. They don't seem to care that the fun they have popping my lice means I can't go and play during breaktime. They don't seem to mind humiliating me in front of everyone with their lice therapy session either. One day, during the long break, the two teachers get into an actual dispute, involving all twenty fingers, as they fight over a plump tick they've found tightly attached to my scalp. "What a bunch of hags", I think to myself.

Almost none of my friends care that I have lice. They understand that with only a hand-operated water pump it's quite difficult to stay clean and keep the lice away from my head.

And then there's my good friend, Marcelo Villagreen. He seems to care a lot. What's worse, we share a desk together in the classroom. Today, at the end of first break, a teacher catches him itching his head and after checking manages to pick out a single, scrawny little lice. As soon as Marcelo returns to the classroom and noisily sits down next to me, I get a loud slap on the cheek and he shouts angrily at me, "You gave me lice, Esteban, I know it!"

That slap hurts my soul more than the sum of every punch I've ever received from grown-ups during my short lifetime. It came from my closest friend after all. It takes me a while to forgive him, though I do understand. Little does Marcelo know that there are often more than just lice living in my hair, but all sorts of fleas and ticks too. I guess if he did know about these other inhabitants with whom I share my head, he wouldn't be sharing a desk with me anymore.

I often wonder whether I'm responsible for the neighbours I keep in my hair. There's no doubt they're misbehaving when they suck my blood, which is pretty nasty, but am I responsible or complicit in such misconduct? Because the bugs are essentially part of me; at the end of the day, I'm the one who gives them warmth and feeds them.

In any case, all these extra lives I'm carrying meet their end each time I can rustle up a few coins to go and get a haircut. I'm sick of the terrible bowl cuts my mum always gives me. I end up resembling Carlitos Balá, a sweet-natured children's television presenter who's really charismatic but looks very silly indeed.

Today I take my coins to a hairdresser on Avenida Centenario, near the train station of Béccar. I walk more than forty blocks in the hot late summer sun of the morning so I'm naturally quite tired and thirsty when I arrive. As I scramble up into the high chair, I explain to the hairdresser, an old man, not particularly kind, what sort of cut I want: John Kennedy style, short on the sides and long on top. Needless to say, within a few minutes, I fall sound asleep. On finishing his work, the hairdresser wakes me up with a little jolt and I look up in the mirror in horror. My whole body jumps in fright and I can't hold back the tears. Blubbering, I ask the man, in broken speech, "Why did you have to shave my head to nothing?"

"Because, young man, your hair was home to so many lice and a thick tick that your head was about to explode!" Seeing me gush even more, he tries to explain to me in a more reassuring tone this time, "Now, as they don't have anywhere to live, you won't have any more bugs biting your head".

I keep sobbing all the same, nothing the hairdresser adds can stop the flow of tears from my disbelieving eyes. He doesn't know what to do with me so in the end he decides to just let me go without charging me for the undesired shave he gave me.

Back in school, just a few days after being slapped by my good friend Marcelo, another hard slap is stamped across my face by the interim new headteacher. Now she's someone who seems to fall prey to unbridled hysteria on a daily basis. I think she's got some problem in her head. It's not just that she paints her face too brightly and looks like a real-life witch, with a strong red hue on her lips, bright blues on her eyelids and more blazing red blotches on her cheeks, but she also wears, every single day, these high leather riding boots, in black or brown, depending on the occasion, through summer and winter alike. Above her boots flap the wings of the white overall every teacher has to wear, unbuttoned and sleeves rolled up. But this token of normality is purely superficial for around her neck hang colourful necklaces strewn with precious stones that seem to possess mysterious properties. There also hangs in the air around her a sour-smelling perfume so potent that occasionally I think I can detect it from the other side of the courtyard.

Her surname is Polsson. It's a name that at first calls to mind the reincarnation of an old English horse-riding lady, but then hearing her voice makes me think more of a mad, frustrated Argentine rider, daughter of some lone rabid wolf of the Pampas. I can't say for sure but I get the feeling all of us students are in agreement: she's a rather vile being, resurrected from hell itself, whose presence we'd be smart to avoid.

One day, I discover the button that rings the loud bell for breaktime. It's a little high for my small stature, but I reckon that, climbing on top of my partner-in-mischief Willy Rodriguez, I'll be able to reach the button and cause a great commotion to the amusement of all my friends.

And so I press it, many times, on many different occasions throughout the term, confusing everyone's notions about breaktime and making the already half-deranged Srta.

Polsson even crazier. Sometimes I even do it when I'm meant to be sitting quietly in class: I only have to ask for urgent permission to use the bathroom and then slip out, followed shortly after by my accomplice Willy.

We manage to avoid getting caught until one afternoon when that hysterical horse-riding headteacher, now close to fever pitch, decides to sit patiently spying on the button behind the long, thick curtain that covers her office window. She catches us red-handed, just as I was up on Willy's shoulders, ready to press the bell.

The headmistress storms over to grab us by the ear and drag us into her lair where we're made to sign the discipline book three times in a row and then sent to stand like vases outside the door to her office, with our foreheads glued to the wall, unable to return to our classroom or even move an inch. How brutish can she be, this woman!

After several hours standing in penance like this, I decide I'm quite bored enough and glance over at Willy, which is enough for the Lucifer inside me to kindle and devise a little more mischief.

When a tall, slender naive-looking girl from Year 8 passes by, I take my chance and say to her quickly, "Excuse me, the headteacher sent me to turn on that light, but I can't reach the switch, it's a bit high for me, you can see I'm very short. Could you turn it on for me, please?"

The girl with the sweet face nods and goes to innocently press the button, which of course is not for the light at all but the break bell. This time the bell rings out for what seems an eternity, during which the headteacher Martha Lylian Polsson comes out of her office fuming like a ferocious wolf hungry and thirsting for blood. The girl immediately points to me saying, "Ma'am, that boy told me you sent him to turn on the light and asked me for help because he couldn't reach the switch."

I'm somehow really hoping my latest prank won't inflict further punishment on me but I'm quickly proved wrong as the crazy, horseback-riding woman walks firmly up to me and without hesitation plants a flat venomous sting on my right cheek, so loud and shocking that I spin round and fall flat on the cold, damp grey floor of the school.

My mother never comes to school, neither for parent meetings nor for any sort of celebration; on the other hand, I don't think my father ever cared about my life right from the very beginning, let alone my upbringing and education. I haven't seen him for a long time and yet today, precisely today, he comes looking for me at school, arriving on the scene minutes after the second bell-ringing incident, the headmistress' blood still boiling with the contempt she feels towards me.

My cheek stinging, and now probably turning purple, the crazed woman approaches my father and says right in front of me, "Your child is recalcitrant to the extreme. I think that he ought not to come back to this school. He should be placed in a reformatory."

I don't understand what 'recalcitrant' means, but the mention of a reformatory sets alarm bells ringing instantly and I burst into angry tears. Furiously I say wicked words to this witch, but my pain isn't over yet as my pitiless father then turns to me, right there in front of the headteacher and my friend Willy, and hands me my third slap of the week, with full force, laying me back onto the cold grey floor again. Painful as it was, at least it hit my left cheek this time. The worst thing of all is that he hit me without even asking what had actually happened, without knowing that the headteacher had already served me my punishment, less than an hour ago, with another brutal slap.

I know that I sometimes misbehave; I honestly don't know why I do it. My mum tells me that I carry a demon inside me, fresh from the *gehinnom* itself, that because of my bad behaviour she'll have a heart attack one day.

I don't understand the obsession some adults have with beating up children. Instead of talking to us gently they hit us; I think it's a big mistake. I'd be much better off if the adults just talked to me instead of beating me, but then again maybe I wouldn't have as much fun.
Sometimes I think that a lot of parents have children but few children have parents. At least it's true in my case. My father abandoned me when I was five years old, he gets angered very easily and is very hard to pacify. He only turns very occasionally just to hit me or give me some kind of punishment, like staring at the wall kneeling on corn.
My father never once told me he loves me. Instead, from time to time, when I do go to stay at his house, he tells me the night before about the beatings he's going to give me in

the morning. I feel so distressed that I can't fall asleep. So I spend the night gripped by a terror that even the prayer from Psalm 91 can't dispel. I dread the coming of dawn and the certain punishment that awaits me.

I begin to imagine he gave up his duties as my father just to protect me from himself, from his monstrous side. It's a comforting thought.

I have frequent nightmares I don't share with anyone because I think they're that type which need to be confronted alone. Even when the unease that results from these nightmares becomes such a burden for me to carry on my own, I have no one with whom to share them. Besides, why talk about them anyway if they're not real? Do I have the right to be loved by my father? Will I ever stop having nightmares? What is the difference between dreams and nightmares?

CHAPTER SIX
Irma
Serious and sagacious

Doña Irma, the ever-serious looking porter, is in charge of serving up the afternoon tea to the two hundred or so students at school.

School is like my second home, sometimes I like going but most of the time I hate it. When grandma Raquel was still around, I almost never skipped school because she used to come and collect me. I was forced out of the front gate only to be kindly escorted back by her.

To be honest, I didn't like grandma Raquel coming into school, not just because I was afraid the teachers would tell her I hadn't done my homework or been very naughty, but because she always came dressed with the same old patched clothing which was all she had, her hair smelling of burnt wood. I felt a bit embarrassed. But now I think her misfortunes in life resonate more with me. After all, I do wear the white overall we were given at the Union, which covers up all the dirt on my skin, patches on my clothes, along with any other aches and misery my body has endured.

I often dream half-awake about silly things like seeing my other Grandma, Berta, coming to collect me from school, elegantly dressed with fur over her shoulders, dazzling in jewellery, her nails painted a soft pink colour. I can see her every night putting curlers in her hair for bed: her hair always has such volume! But it's only a dream. She's never even been to my school or to our little shack. I think she often forgets that I exist.

On the day grandma Raquel's hit by the car on Avenida Marquez, mum comes home and hangs up the overcoat she's been wearing, now stained with blood, on a nail hammered into the wall. Right next to it, at the very entrance of the house, there's a large mysterious key Grandma hung up the day before she left the house that morning.

The overcoat hangs there for several days after she's gone and my eyes swell up every time they fall on it. I touch it and smell it, my tears being absorbed as I mourn her absence. I suddenly feel ashamed for having been ashamed of her. I know I can no longer ask her for forgiveness. Oh how dearly I miss her! I want to kiss and hug her but it's too late because she's gone. She went to heaven.

At home we have the manual pump to draw water, that same green one from Grand Bourg, which gives us the freshest natural water from the depths of the earth, so ideal for preparing *yerba mate* tea, as my mum says. But we still have no tank, no pipes, no drains, no boiler, no heating, no toilet, no bidet, no sink to wash dishes or hands, let alone a washing machine, dryer, iron or any of those modern appliances.

One day the teachers send all of us students for a medical check-up. They say it's an order from the Ministry of Education. I've been told to go to Colegio Marín, a huge school on Avenida del Libertador, in San Isidro. It's the same school where my paternal ancestors Giuseppe and his brother Michelle worked when they first came to Argentina from Jonadi, Italy. I turn up at the medical office, accompanied by my friend Guillermo Carreras and his mother.

After a long wait, I'm called in for my examination. The elderly doctor beckons me in and proceeds to check me for everything imaginable. He first has me undress completely, gently taps at my knees with a wooden hammer to check the reflex, inspects the numerous cavities in my teeth, looks down my throat, examines my toes, bum and willy. He weighs me on the scales, places something round on my chest, and then my back, which is connected up to his ears; I think it's called a stethoscope. It's quite cold on my skin and gives me a tickle. He then asks me to say "thirty-three" out loud. I don't know why that number and not another number, but I just say it anyway without asking.

Finally he takes silent look at my fingernails, squeezes my neck with his fingers like he is looking for something, and sits down to write for a while. At length, he looks up and says to me, "You're as fit as you are filthy. Next time, before coming to the doctor, have a wash, why don't you? Get under the hot shower and have a good scrub with some soap. Understand?"

"Yes, Señor Doctor, I understand", I say sheepishly, looking down at my feet, feeling the same rush of blood to my cheeks I usually get when challenged by grown-ups.

He ends my health assessment by asking if I've ever had mumps, rubella, smallpox or chickenpox. I've never had any of those funny named diseases; I don't know what they are, so I shake my head each time. He then scribbles in the booklet, stamps and signs it, hands it back to me and grudgingly bids me off saying "Goodbye, little sir."

It's quite clear to me that Sr. Doctor was unhappy with my filthy state. Luckily for him at least, as I'm unintentionally bald now, I don't have any lice with which to inconvenience his work. I can't avoid feeling the hurt that this silly man of science did to me with his words though.

He asked me to do something I'd no doubt very much like to, but I simply can't because we don't have a shower. I haven't taken one for months. It's hard enough just having a simple wash!

First we have to go fetch some dry firewood from the strip of land along the Pan-American Highway, loading it onto our shoulders and tying it up with a stray piece of string or cable. Needless to say, carrying that weight is quite a tough task for my small frame. Anyway, we lumber back and stack up the wood outside the house, far enough away so as not to set it alight.

Once the fire is lit we fill a large, old Shell barrel with water and put it on an iron triangle with legs at each joint, which was made for us by the lads in the municipal workshop. Mum calls it a tripod.

With the water now bubbling, the next step is to use a bucket to mix it with some cold water in a big zinc container that serves as our bathtub. When the temperature is just right we can hop in and pour the water over our heads with a little aluminium can. It's a tedious process that becomes even more so on cold rainy winter days.

During that time of year, it's hard enough just finding dry firewood. To save having to get more and more of it, we use the same water for all of us. Uncle Marcelo also gets the first bath. When it's my turn the water is already quite dirty, but with a final rinse I come out clean enough.

Mum's rule is that you don't have to throw away the dirty water until you have clean water. She applies a similar rule to other stuff too, like when something breaks, there's no point throwing it out until we have a replacement. Sometimes I take a bath once a week but it's usually every two weeks. And I never shower.

That doctor had every right to ask me to come in nice and clean for the health check-up, and yet I don't have the right to a shower. Mum often says that being poor doesn't mean being dirty, to which I reply, "It doesn't mean *being* dirty, Mama, but *living* dirty". I use the two different verbs for 'being' in Spanish, *ser* and *estar*, to proudly make my point. It's true I've been passionate about the intricacies of language from an early age, even if there are hundreds of words that still puzzle me.

Mum doesn't believe that to be poor is a natural condition of human beings, as if imposed by God, nor does she resign herself, as some inevitably do, to poverty. Instead she thinks that being poor is *unnatural*, even more so in a rich country like Argentina, and that God doesn't want us to stay poor, that we must strive to cease our poverty, to progress in life…

I know that I'm still a kid, but I'm not so young as to not understand how easy it is to resign yourself to the life that landed in your lap, perhaps by destiny. I can also confess it becomes even trickier to escape when there are other, better lives right next to you, like the one they have in grandma Berta's house or in any of the great mansions surrounding my shack.

My mother decides, one day, to build the first brick wall at the entrance to the plot where we live. Then she hires a bricklayer to complete the job.

A man comes to take up the task, with his son Luis acting as a labourer on the construction.
Luis is 25 years old, an attractive and virile young man. He smiles all the time at my mum and his eyes are full of desire, his torso bare and glistening with sweat as he passes the bricks to his father. Within a few weeks he moves in to our house, and after another nine months I'm put to work helping out Mum: she's about to have her first child with her second husband. For the second time in her life, she believes in love.
Luis soon turns out to be a virtually non-existent, lazy alcoholic husband. He too beats my mother up, just as my own father did.
These men, they humiliate my mum, threaten her, appear to

despise her, and she endures it all in silence, drowning in the shame of having picked two wrong sorts in a row, and feeling unable to escape from them. She suffers just like many other women do who live in this male-dominated, tailor-made world.

It seems to be a world made hell for women, since they're not treated as equals and don't own their freedom. In our country abuse is common; divorce is illegal and separation seen in a very poor light. My mother leapt out of the frying pan and into the fire, consequently dragging me with her.

No doubt she needs help, especially when Luis hits her, but what can I do against such a big, muscular man.

I once told him not to beat her up anymore and he said to me with a grave tone and threatening gestures, "Stay out of adult matters, you little shit, or I'll leave your arse looking like the flag of Japan."

My mother must master the deep fear she harbours—she must not allow terror to dominate her—and yet I notice that she already finds it very difficult to bear the burden. I feel so powerless to help her.

No son likes to see his mother beaten up but I don't know what I can do, other than perhaps confront this ogre of a man and try to subdue him with words alone.

This is why I love my mother: for her bravery and her sacrifice. Not simply because she carried me for nine months in her womb, but because despite all the trials she is put through, she is always present, by my side, offering me love and taking care of me the best she can; the abuse goes unspoken, ever veiled under a code of familiar silence about which nobody speaks and it needs to be hidden.

Thank God, his presence is not constant, but his disappearances are: when he comes, he is usually drunk and, after putting together violent scenes, he simply vanishes.

When I get home, after that traumatic visit to the doctor, I decide that taking a shower doesn't have to be so impossible at all. I find an old watering can, fill it up and thread it onto one of the low-hanging branches of the tall willow tree at the back of the house, tying some rope around the watering can's neck so that when I pull it the water comes out just like the shower that the doctor told me about.

But my first experience of modern hygiene is suddenly cut short when a host of hairy caterpillars (actually known as hairy *cats*!), *hylesia nigricans*, are inadvertently shaken out of the willow branches above me, showering down on my back. This is my first and last shower with this ingenious invention in the warm summer of Buenos Aires. Those hairy caterpillars leave me with painful red welts all over my body: it is the price of cleanliness that I pay just to be able to take a shower as the doctor ordered me.

I curse the doctor for being so inconsiderate and not wondering first about where and how I live. If he had, I wouldn't have thought of the idea of taking a shower in the first place and the *hylesia nigricans* wouldn't have stung me. It occurs to me that there are inept doctors around here who don't ask the right questions, who don't listen to their patients, and instead of helping us they just pile on more harm, on top of what we're already carrying on our shoulders.

Back in school, we have a new headteacher, Srta. Elena, and we now get to have refreshments and sometimes even a snack. I don't know how she manages to make it happen but she seems so kind, and so different from that crazy horse-riding lady that slapped me a few times. She puts enough money together so that every day, during the long break, each student can have something hot to drink; it might be stewed *yerba mate* with milk one day and *cascarilla* with milk the next.

The first one, whose scientific name is Ilexparaguariensis, you boil in water and then add milk and sugar. The second, also known as *croton eluteria*, consists of chippings of brown bark, whose tree I've never come across, which is also boiled in water and has a flavour and aroma similar `to chocolate.

When ready, Irma stands in the covered patio stirring a large pot on top of a chair with a ladle made of aluminium in her right hand. We then line up carrying our own cups. She fills everyone's cup, and there's no going back for more. Occasionally, however, I sneak to the back of the queue and tiptoe my way back to her innocently. She pretends not to have noticed and is always willing to pour a second helping in my cup, also made of aluminium.

88

Monday mornings are even more special as a local bakery kindly donates to the school their sweet pastries left over from the weekend. They're a little old but I think they're delicious. My favourite things are *tortitas negras,* (doughnuts topped with brown sugar), *sacramentos* (mini-croissants filled with quince), *bolas de fraile* (literally, 'friar's balls'; doughnuts stuffed with toffee), *medialunas* ('half-moon' croissants), and *vigilantes* (long thin croissants).

Where did they get the curious names for the Argentine pastries? Based on what are things named?

CHAPTER SEVEN
Isabel
President and harassed

I've been working in Lolita's grocery store for a long time now, stocking the fridges before school, but if I want to make a little more, I'm going to have to look further afield as well.

My first thought is to become a salesman, although I don't think I quite have the spark required to sell things like the Chinese do; on TV, people are always saying they're capable of selling you anything, even fake stuff.

As I sift through rubbish I pick up all sorts of old junk: toys, marbles and stamps of every saint under the sun. One day I find the stamp of San Cayetano and immediately think it must be very valuable because I remember people on TV saying that he's the one who gives work to the unemployed who pray to him each year. I've heard how there are endless queues to enter the church dedicated to him in the *barrio* of Liniers.

Finding San Cayetano himself so unexpectedly amongst the rubbish feels like a miracle to me and I bring him home with a big smile. Of course, I'd have to sell it for a high price, minimum fifty cents, enough at least to buy me two 'Topolin' lollipops with their surprises.

Mum doesn't like at all my collection of saints and virgins rescued from the rubbish. She says that it's *idolatry* and that the saints have eyes yet don't see, hands yet don't feel, ears yet don't listen, mouths yet don't speak or eat, noses yet don't smell. But even if the saints do have all those disabilities I still think I can make a bit of money out of them, so long as Mum doesn't get her hands on them first and throw them back into the rubbish. I have to hide them away at night and then during the day I go and stand out on the pavement in front of the house trying to sell them to passersby. No one is interested though. Somewhat disheartened, I take a seat on an old tree trunk that grandma Raquel gave and looked after for many years when it was still part of a living tree.

I don't know why Mum cut it down one day; I love it because it connects me to grandma Raquel.

I love all trees for that matter, because of how they die, most of the time, standing up; this one in particular, however, did not die standing but was axed down by the tenacious hand of my mother.

Anyhow, I decide to stick to my new job, using an upside-down empty box of Argentinean apples as a counter to display my products, among which there's my collection of saints and virgins of course, a TV Guide, two copies of *Radiolandia*, one of *El Gráfico* and another of *Selections from Reader's Digest*. All of them show a little wear and tear; one has two famous boxers on its cover, Ringo Bonavena and Carlos Monzón, another the magnificent racing car driver Juan Manuel Fangio.

Added to these are lots of *Paturuzú* comics that my uncle Marcelo gave me, a small and varied army of toy soldiers, a wooden spoon that I decorated at school one day for Mother's Day, and an ashtray that I made out of an unscented white loaf of soap for Father's Day that's next to useless because I practically don't have a dad anyway, nor do I know if he even smokes or not.

Also up for sale are a few germinating beans from a school project where we put some blotting paper in a jar with some sand in the middle and three white beans wedged between damp paper and the glass.

It was a worthwhile experiment since the beans are already sprouting and looking now quite healthy with their green shoots and leaves: it's been a very promising crop this time round. Other times the beans usually end up drenched and rotten from the excessive amounts of water I anxiously give them. Not this time. They look fresh, green and happy to be alive; genuinely using their leaves to carry out the process of photosynthesis, which the teachers are so insistent for us to learn in school.

My sale begins at 5.30pm, just after I've finished school and had some milky *mate cocido* and a piece of bread. People slowly potter by, taking the odd look at my humble wares. They all smile but nobody buys a thing.

The only person who shows any sincere interest in my goods is Don Braulio, the local sharpener who passes by our house around six o'clock every Thursday on his bicycle, announcing his approach by blowing on a funny looking instrument. He pulls up and says to me, "Hey Poroto, what are you up to?"
"I've started a business selling second hand items. What are you doing?"

"I'm looking for things to sharpen."

"Like what?"

"Anything with an edge really… Scissors, knives, razors, anything sharp."

"Will you let me play on your harmonica, if that's what it is?"

"It's not a harmonica, it's a 'pan flute' and the sound it makes is called a *chiflo*."

Unaware of any other meanings for the word '*pan*', I ask, "How can it possibly be *bread* if I can clearly see it's made of wood?"

"No, no," he says, "Pan is the name given to the instrument, in honour of a Greek god called Pan who played a flute like this one blowing along the tops of the pipes which make deeper notes the longer they are and vice versa."

Humph. Once again an adult is leaving me confused using too many strange words together and talking about musical gods. I decide to change the subject and ask him, "This bike, did you make it?"

"No, it's a normal bike. I just built a mechanical grinder with a sharpening stone onto the back of it. So when I pedal, the stone spins around really fast and I can sharpen almost anything people give me. You try to make a living every day selling second-hand stuff and I do so by sharpening."

"Well, anyhow, you're distracting me now, Don Braulio", I tell him firmly but with a smile, "I'm not going to sell anything if you hang around here talking".

He wishes me luck with my business and pedals away. Before I know it I'm slowly nodding off as I sit there on grandma Raquel's tree trunk with my head resting on a ramshackle wooden fence. I wake up confused the next morning in the bed I share with Mum. Before I can say anything, she explains to me that a good salesman never falls asleep at work because bad people can come along and rob him and sink his business.

I blush and then ask her, worried, "And San Cayetano, and the other saints, where are they?"

"The devil took them, Satan", she replies. It's not clear to me if she used 'devil' and 'Satan' as synonyms, or whether she was actually calling *me* Satan. I dare not ask either. I'd rather shut up and avoid starting the day with another fight.

Today is 24th March and Mum and I are off to do the shopping. We walk to the supermarket called *Rincón*, the first one to appear in the neighbourhood, on Avenida Rolón that follows on from the same Avenida Márquez where grandma Raquel died a few years before. Just when we're rounding the church of Santa Rita, Mum turns to me and says, "Son, today the military threw out Isabelita, and they've now appointed themselves rulers of the country, I'm quite concerned about what might happen, what they're going to do with her and what comes next."

When we arrive at the supermarket everyone's talking about a *coup*; some people are elated and others, like my mum, stay silent, though I can tell they're distraught. We go home and turn the TV on to find all the shows are different. Some are saying that the military has finally decided to take power and that with them the nation will finally know peace and order.

Mum explains that the military has made a habit out of doing evil and that, in a total frenzy, they're *disappearing* all those who oppose them. She goes on to tell me that they kicked President Isabelita Perón out of the Casa Rosada when there were only six months left for her to finish her term in office. She teaches me that what they did is called a *coup d'etat*, a word that comes from French and sounds rather nice and elegant but actually involves horrendous barbarity. She says they've formed a military junta whereby they appoint each other president rotating in and out of office every few years. "This is very bad, son, and it's going to end even worse", she tells me. I listen to her words very carefully, surprised by everything I'm hearing. She seems very agitated and is talking non-stop. She explains that it's as if the military has gone crazy and the madness is spreading like a virus.

There are people who are civilians and yet they like the military and support them, so it's better not to talk politics with anyone.

A few months on and it becomes clear these people weren't wrong: the military indeed bring about 'order', in the form of the "National Reorganisation Process", in which they re-organise everything, to such an extent that we soon begin to fear all this order. They impose the death penalty and I start to hear their slogan repeated on TV almost every day, such as "*Achicar el Estado es agrandar a la Nación*" (to shrink the state is to enlarge the nation), and many other new things I haven't come across before and don't understand either.

I grow up under this military rule with alternating presidents, starting with Videla, followed by Viola, Galtieri and Bignone. All but one with moustaches and boots; and one is quite clearly an alcoholic, too.

One cold dark evening, the sun well hidden by now, returning from a firewood collection trip, a few meters from our house, at the entrance to the school, we find a very old woman (probably close to a hundred years old in my estimation) curled up on the floor under an old frayed poncho.

Mum speaks to her and there's no answer, she doesn't seem to be breathing. Mum then rubs her back to see if she can rouse her. It's freezing out here and it's as if the woman is slowly dying in front of us, but suddenly her sad and tired eyes creak open. She says she no longer has a house, at which point Mum tells her we're going to take her to our shack.

We help her up and walk with her very slowly. She has her left arm around Mum's back and rests her right hand on my shoulder using me like a cane. I notice her cold hands are covered with chilblains.

Once back inside home, Mum prepares a delicious steaming

chicken broth that she serves into an aluminium bowl and gives to the old granny, before pouring me some too. Our guest slurps the hot liquid in desperation and after a few minutes her lips break into a broad smile, all gum and no teeth; that smile is the most beautiful smile I've yet seen in my short life.

She tells us that her name is Clara Suarez, that she went out early to beg this morning and fell victim to the cold while sitting on the portal to my school. Mum tells her she can stay with us for the night and offers her my new bed.

So that night I share Mum's bed again and she hugs me tenderly in the dark whispering into my ear that it's our duty to help the poor, the beggars, and especially the elderly. She says that widows, prisoners and orphans must all be given a hand. There's no reason why we should let a day go by without giving something to someone and it's an even better deed to help out a stranger. Besides, giving to an unknown person its better, because can eradicate that feeling of pride people sometimes get when they give. I can't grasp much of what she says and soon I drift off into a deep sleep in her arms, just the way I like it. I love sleeping with Mum by my side because I no longer fear getting lost or meeting some nasty death in the night. By the time I wake up, grandma Clara has already left, without saying goodbye, just as grandma Raquel left, without saying goodbye.

Many things are changing rapidly across the country thanks

to the *milicos*, as the military in government are now called. I experience some of this change first-hand. It begins when I hear a neighbour, who has an acquaintance who's a cousin of a friend of a colonel, commenting in Lolita's grocery store that the government is ordering the closure of the local Community Centre around the corner from my house.

As I work in the grocery store in the mornings, I'm in the perfect position to listen in on the exchange of information about everything going on in the neighbourhood. And now, right here in front of the counter I'm wiping down, this man comes along and says that the Community Centre on Calle Jacinto Díaz, at the corner of Barbosa, has just been closed down because it "threatens order and public safety".
I spread the news to my friends in the neighbourhood and we all decide to continue using the Community Centre in secret. So it is that we meet there every evening: Guille, Gerardo (who we call Pupo (belly button) because his father was known as Don Puppo and had his name painted on the door of a large green truck he owned), Gallego, occasionally two of the triplets, Marcelo and me, Poroto Fasule Garbanzo (my full nickname, a mixture of legumes that each emphasise my diminutive stature).

We creep in through a window that's never any trouble to open and once inside the fun really starts: we play cops and robbers, marbles, cards, and sometimes more serious games like the lottery, or a card game called "Stealing Bundles".

All this keeps us well entertained for a good while until one late afternoon our luck runs out and a green Ford Falcon car, followed by a truckload of *milicos,* pull up like something out of Operation Swat, the series on TV, and break into the Community Centre.

There are around twenty soldiers in green uniforms, all with helmets on their heads. They smash open the door, breaking it off its hinges, and immediately order us out of the playroom and into the backyard where they have us lie on our faces.

I feel a heavy black boot on my delicate spine and see out of the corner of my eye a rifle pointing at my head. All of us are terrified. I'm trembling like a leaf in the middle of a storm, only just managing to hold back my tears. I cannot, however, hold back my bladder and I start to feel the warmth spreading under my legs. Such an unhappy surprise causes me to flush red with shame. A voice then orders us to our feet and the soldiers start to search us, patting down our bodies. The one in front of me looks absolutely disgusted and does his best not to touch my wet patches. We are then each given a hard kick up the backside, following which a fat moustachioed man calls out, "You ill-bred brats! Get back to your dens immediately and never come here again! Is that fucking clear?"
"Yes, sir," we respond, almost in unison, and off we run to our homes.

This is the first of a few altercations I have with the military. Even though I did read 'The Little Prince', one of the books now banned by the military, I don't think I'm very political, revolutionary, subversive, or anything of those other ghastly things they say on TV, like a guerilla fighter and a communist.

I'm simply Poroto Fasule Garbanzo, just a silly kid who goes to school in a white overall. The only naughty thing I sometimes do is sing to my General the *Marcha Peronista*.

Sometimes under that same bridge, Blanco Encalada, where I go to sing my heart out, they organise illegal car races up to Tomkinson Bridge. One Saturday night, we find there's nothing much to do at home as our electricity has been cut off for not having paid the bill on time. We have a perfectly good kerosene lamp, of course, which gives off plenty of light, but we do get a bit bored without the TV.

The sound of cars racing down the Pan-American Highway is far too enticing for us to turn down.

Mum tells Marcelo, me and my older brother Daniel, who's visiting for the weekend, that the car races are extremely dangerous to attend and that we're forbidden to go out and watch them at all costs.

It's a beautiful, warm summer night, already getting on close to midnight; Mum is in a deep sleep, shattered as ever, still coping with the death of Grandma, which has resulted in the onset of progressive deafness with psychological implications that prevent her from hearing anything without a hearing aid. This time she closed the house door earlier, locking the chain and hiding away the key, but given her deep, soundless sleep I'm sure she won't make out anything untoward.

It occurs to me that we can still slip off to watch the races through the window. It's the only one we have and, fortunately, it now lies open to mitigate some of the heat that has filled up the house during the day.

There's also a stuffy smell of incense inside emanating from three green spirals sticking out of empty glass bottles of Coca Cola and Orange Crush that we use to keep at bay the battalions of mosquitoes that assail us every night.

My occasional allies, Marcelo and Daniel, agree to my plan and we slowly squeeze through the window one by one and head towards the highway. There, on top of Tomkinson Bridge, we find a very amusing sight: the whole place is full of adults, and a few young people too, shouting and applauding. We start betting with marbles on which car is going to win. Suddenly a red Peugeot 504 going at full speed starts to spin out of control. Daniel, who knows something about mechanics, says car has *differential problems*. I take from this that the car is different and can't cope with the speed following the curve of the bridge, and that's why it's sent spinning, making many spectators scream in fright. We instinctively fill the air with noisy enthusiasm, and the applause is further unleashed when the driver is thrown free from the vehicle without a *rasguño*, or scratch. That's the word they use. I don't know why but I really like this particular word.

It brings to mind the scratches that cats give you with their claws; I can't get my head around how the driver of the car could have possibly been attacked by a cat. Anyhow I find it all hilarious and it gets even more fun when a convoy of military trucks, Jeeps and green Ford Falcon cars appear on the bridge. The soldiers immediately start shooting people from the vehicles and suddenly the air is once again full of screams, no longer enthusiastic but desperate. Some people end up really hurt, but fortunately no one dies. It seems like I've witnessed a true miracle. Daniel later explains to me that in these cases the soldiers are known to use rubber bullets, which are very painful but not mortal.

We get away by hiding in the long grass at the side of the Highway, where we stay until the whole mess is over. Those who can't run away in time end up in the back of the military trucks. Who knows what fate awaits them.

Thankful to have survived our daring escapade, we slip back in through a window and quietly slide into bed. One more surprise, however, awaits us: Mum's figure emerges from the darkness like a lioness ready to strike, armed with a willow branch still firm and supple. She begins whipping us savagely. Marcelo yells out begging her, "No, stop hitting me, please!"
Daniel also implores her, "Mama, forgive me, please, forgive us."
I, on the other hand, have no desire to quell her anger, resolving to make matters far worse by wildly shouting out

all sorts of rude things at her, "You are a witch! You're a horrible mother". The more I insult her, the more she thrashes me. At the time, I don't know why I'm always the one who gets whipped the most. It doesn't take much reflection to work out later that it's probably because I disrespect her; I find it so hard to just shut up like the others do and this makes her even angrier. Soon I feel a great sense of shame for my behaviour and begin to deeply regret having been so disrespectful to her.

According to my mum, I'm always the one to blame for any disasters at home. I like being called an *initiator* because it sounds a bit like a *doctor*, which is like someone in the hospital where Mum works. Marcelo calls me a snake, while mother calls me a scoundrel, an evil one. "You carry the devil inside you, son", she tells me over and over.
I love my mother very much. I really do appreciate and value the great sacrifice she makes to raise me, but I can't stand it when she grinds me down to nothing. She is hard to anger and easy to pacify but when she grinds me down she does it with such ease.

Before going to bed every night, I leave out a mug, a teaspoon, the sugar jar and the kettle full of water, all prepared on the table, so that Mum can have a cup of tea as soon as she gets up in the morning at four and gets ready to go to work. If I find any biscuits or a piece of bread, I put it next to the teacup and cover it with a towel.

Mum loves some peace and quiet when she returns

shattered from work in the evening. Every day she has to wash down the white patio, the bathrooms, the ward, the pharmacy, the offices and who knows how many other floors. She has to do everything just right because her boss Srta. Alba is an informant for the military person that the new government put in hospitals as directors. So if Mum arrives late or does something wrong Srta. Alba can get angry and suspend her. She also fears more than ever losing her attendance bonus and ending up making less money, which is a worrying prospect for me too as I'm always hungry and all we eat at home is rice and hard bread. I'm always hoping someone will pay us a visit and bring something tasty.

I sometimes find the Municipal Hospital a good distraction from the boredom and hunger at home. I often go there to meet Mum at the end of her shift, walking the thirty or so blocks, consumed by my daydreams.

Sometimes when I'm sick and Mum doesn't want to leave me at home alone she even takes me with her to the hospital where I follow her around as she goes about her work. It turns out other times I actually have to go, like when I'm bitten by a stray dog one day: a nurse who works with Mum called Elvira gives me 40 rabies shots in 40 days. She also talks with a funny lisp so I know she must be Spanish, like Don Justo.
Another time I'm playing with my cousin Liliana one day and a heavy iron seesaw suddenly catches my right thumb in the wrong place at the wrong time splitting it right open.

Ouch. They rush me in to the emergency room where Dr. Marcovecchio sews up my thumb with five stitches.

And only a few days later, I'm back again to see Dr. Marcovecchio; this time it's more serious. My brother Daniel is playing around as a gardener in the backyard with a double-headed hoe, which has a digging blade on one side and a two-pronged fork on the other. He's trying to plant some pumpkin seeds, but I want to use it to finish digging my tunnel to Australia.

It's just that I saw on the globe on the teacher's desk at school that Argentina was right opposite Australia and so I want to go looking for some kangaroos! I've already dug a hole about my height in depth, but I know I have a long way to go to get to Sydney.

Mum watches on, full of tenderness, as I dig away this first part and asks me a favour. I assent, and then she says to me, "I'd be extremely grateful if, before arriving in Australia, you could stop by Jerusalem to leave a little prayer in the Western Wall."
"Your wish is my command, Mum." I reply without hesitating, though I'm somewhat puzzled. Does she mean that I have to learn to speak to a wall? That can't be right.
She senses from the growing look of confusion on my face that I'm lost and adds, "It's a huge wall in Israel where you can post letters to God." It's still a little strange to me but I go along with it, talking to stones.

Anyway, as I was saying, my brother is now working the land and he's totally ignoring me. I repeat my request for the hoe, explaining that I have to keep digging my hole because I now have to get to Jerusalem and it's urgent, but he doesn't listen to me.

Frustrated at his disregard for me, I approach him from behind and make to give him a push, just as he's raising the hoe to strike down again. He doesn't know I'm behind him. The two prongs are stuck into my head and withdrawn in an instant, leaving two little holes that instantly stream jets of blood. I begin to feel very dizzy and collapse to the ground.

Mum runs over to me despairing, covers my head with a towel and, from our neighbour Telma's phone, calls the hospital for an ambulance. One arrives in no time and I'm quickly stretchered on board. Travelling like this is pretty fun, it feels like I'm in a Hollywood film. The only thing is I'm in a lot of pain and too stunned to fully embrace this new adventure.

I arrive at the hospital, still semi-conscious, and I'm wheeled into the emergency room I know so well. I make out the same hoarse and truculent voice of Dr. Marcovecchio as he gives me an anti-tetanus injection. He then gives me something to dilute the intense pain I'm in and sets about fitting two metal pieces into each of the holes in my head, closing them shut. I can still feel a lot of what they're doing on my head so Elvira and Mum are holding my body tightly. I kick and scream making all sorts of fuss; it's a miracle they don't end up making the wound worse! Those two little metal plugs manage to close the holes in no time. Two weeks later they're taken out for good. I like to have metal on my head, I feel like a bionic human with two antennae ready to contact aliens.

For me, the problem now becomes the bandage, because I still have two protruding lumps on my head, which look like a pair of fledgling horns. At school, some of the kids from Year 8 start calling me a *cuckold*; while my own classmates say it's like I now have two donkey ears similar to the ones handed out by our laudable former headteacher, Srta. Polsson, to anyone in school who doesn't know what they ought to know.

A month later and I'm back in the hospital, this time for the harmless reason of spending another day working alongside my mum. Today she is needed in the morgue; we walk in to find a beautiful girl laid out, lifeless, dressed for her wedding. I hear that it was the result of an accident, that when she went to get married in the Cathedral of San Isidro she was in a hurry and didn't want to make her groom wait for her; she sped along in the back of a car finely adorned with flowers and white ribbons, which then zigzagged its way around the lowered train barriers of Belgrano Street, just a few meters from the station.
The train called Bartolomé Mitre struck the car, killing the lovely bride instantly. The customers crowded around the nearby hot dog stand "Coquito" rushed over to her side but recognised immediately that nothing could be done for her. She was brought to the morgue, her once white dress now

soaked in red. Srta. Alba wanted my mother to wipe the blood from the girl's face so that her family might recognise her.

And so I follow my mother in; curiously, there's no smell of death in the air. However, the mere sight of this unhappy bride makes me cry uncontrollably. Mum closes the girl's eyes so that she can rest in peace and leave her sadness behind. She explains to me that what we see before us is only a body, but that the real person is now in heaven with grandma Raquel. This thought comforts me and draws me closer to death, that I too might visit my Grandma.

Mum is always charged with washing the blood of the injured and deceased, which spills across the floor. Today I turn up unannounced to find her on her knees, scrubbing with a coarse brush along the joints of the white courtyard tiles. It is a sight that moves me deeply.
I wonder how long she'll have to keep on scrubbing the floors of this hospital on her knees. What does it mean to be on your knees?

CHAPTER EIGHT
Mirakle
Radiant and sparkling

Now let us go back to the very beginning for I am yet to give some details of those earliest days.

It so happens that I was born interrupting the day of rest on the third day of the month of miracles and wonders. I saw the light at the Municipal Hospital of La Falda, in the Sierras de Córdoba, at the very heart of the Argentine Confederation.

Of course, I don't remember what happened that Saturday, but Mum tells me some time later that she was eighteen years old at the time, that her pregnancy went very smoothly, that I was the fruit of love and passion shared between her and my father, and that I was conceived at the end of a warm February. I grew and grew in her belly until nine months later when I was finally born in a white hospital under the red-tiled roof of a neat little gable.

She also tells me she arrived at the hospital at noon, accompanied by my father in a black taxi from La Cumbre; that in the back of that taxi the little sac in her belly with me inside it broke, and that the whole car ended up soaking wet. She says that I popped out exactly forty minutes past one in the afternoon.

She goes on to say that I was born the natural way: no need for the doctors to open her belly or use any strange metal tools such as forceps and the like. My father signed a bit of paper that said I exist and that I'm his rightful son.
Even as a baby she thought that I had a friendly face, albeit ugly, red and wrinkly, as if born an old man, and that there

was a pleasant, recently varnished-like smell around me.

I can't remember a lot about those days, but I do remember that in the Sierras de Córdoba we lived well, in a nice well-built house on Calle Corrientes, under another red-tiled roof, mosaic flooring, fully installed bathroom, gas stove in the kitchen, and all the hot and cold taps you could imagine. I also remember seeing snow for the first time, in the Plaza 25 de Mayo, a main square right in front of our house. The snow was whitest white and cold, but beautiful, so very beautiful.

I was about five years old when the disaster befell our little family. It was the figurative hecatomb of my childhood. I didn't want to meddle in my parents' affairs, but these sad and ugly days were coming at us hard and fast, leaving the seven years of marriage built together by Mum Ester and Dad Pedro in total rubble.

When she finds out he's cheating on her, she flies into a fit. So he decides to make fun of her and insult her; then one day, while we're eating, he even throws food at her. He starts to beat her again. She cries. His anger reaches its climax and he simply abandons us, going back to Betty, a hardy young blonde from the area. Mum packs all our clothes into a few bags and we take the bus to Buenos Aires, 770 kilometres south-east. There we move into the precarious little shed grandma Raquel has just put up, on a plot of land she's slowly paying for in a trickle of installments. She had to leave her former home in Martínez due to family inheritance issues. That was the story of my beginning.

Today I'm home alone; Mum's at work, Marcelo's at school, and I'm playing truant again to watch 'Lunch with Mirtha Legrand'. After the show ends, I head outside to play around with the dogs.

I suddenly look up and there before me stands my dad. It's the second time he's shown up during this first year in the shack.

Though I'm initially quite stunned to see him, there's soon a smile across my face. Then I start to feel a little embarrassed as he looks around at the poverty we now live in with Mum; because he turned up unannounced everything is even more messy than usual.

He tells me he only came to invite me to go see the rabbit hatchery he's set up. He explains that he has hundreds of them, all of a good breed, and that he's selling them. He says he knows how much I like taking care of animals and that he thinks I'm going to love seeing them. I'm slightly suspicious because there's no way he can know that: he doesn't know me one bit.

Without wasting any time he motions me into his black Siam Di Tella 1500 and drives me off to a faraway place called Del Viso, in the Province of Buenos Aires. The place sounds like *guiso* to me, a stew, but I say nothing. There my father lives with his new wife called Titina, his third;

she's from Córdoba like me, and an alcoholic like herself.

As soon as we arrive at my father's new home, this woman tells me that I have to call her *Mum* now. Then they take me to see the rabbits, something I end up doing alone on a lot of other occasions as well. Daniel, my older brother is already staying here; he arrived a few days before me and has already started school, at the same place I'm enrolled in. I refuse to go. I just want to go back to my shack to be with my real mum and my dogs.

I don't want to see rabbits any more. I don't want to call Titina my mum. I don't want to eat there, I don't want to play there nor even take a shower there. I cry and cry and cry, for more than a month actually, day and night. I miss the magical kisses my mum used to give me so that I wouldn't have nightmares; I certainly don't miss my father's kisses or his caresses because one can't miss what one never had.

All the while, Mum doesn't know where I am. On the day of my abduction she comes back from work as usual but can't find me at home, so she goes out looking for me at neighbours' houses, the hospital, and the police station, everywhere. She almost has a heart attack and grows more desperate every day, asking anyone and everyone of my whereabouts. Grandma Berta tells her she doesn't know where Estebancito is either, but she's lying; she knows full well of my kidnapping and where I'm being held captive, but she keeps quiet, acting as an accomplice to the thief of a man she raised.

My aversion to this place is deepening, especially the hatchery, where the rabbits are packed by the hundreds into the artificial burrows built by my dad's hands. It's a real dump and the stench is unbearable. The burrows are stock full of newborn bunnies; there are seemingly more of them every hour, with too few parents to look after them. I remember with tainted nostalgia what my mum taught me: animals shouldn't be made to suffer in cages or chains and one should give them food and water before tending to one's own needs. Recalling these words and her voice only serves to upset me even more.

One day my tears swirl me into a blind rage and I sneak off to the hatchery. The rabbits come hopping out cheerfully towards the sunlight and there I am waiting for them like a wolf, ready to snap their necks, only it doesn't seem to be me, it's someone else: maybe the demon they say that's inside of me.

I grab a handful of newborn bunnies and hurl them with what little strength I have against the wall, mercilessly killing them through my own pain. They crack and split. I hate them all. I hate my father, my new 'mum' Titina, and all the damn rabbits in here—they're the real reason I was deceived. They have their mothers and, under the authority of my father, they all conspired to steal me away from my own mother.

Most of the time I do want to dot the i's and cross the t's, and normally I refrain from such outbursts, but not today. Today I just can't control myself and I call Titina all sorts of nasty things, bitch, crazy, drunk, gold digger; I take advantage of the mess and confusion I've just made to escape from my captors. I've no idea how I'm going to find my mum though. I stop by a grocery called El Andaluz to ask for directions to the train station.

At the station the guard tells me to take a train to Boulogne. On arrival at the station, I immediately recognise the train, it's the same one I took with my mother the day we went to pick up the green water pump.
I board the train without a ticket and eventually, somehow, make it home, putting an end to this horrible saga.

The reunion with my mum is one of the tenderest moments I can remember. I walk into the shack and hug her tightly; I burst into tears making sobbing noises that sound like hiccups as I squeeze her. Her cheeks are wet too, and she can't stop kissing and holding me tenderly in her arms.

Another year goes by and one day Mum takes me with her to visit a law firm in downtown San Isidro where we have a meeting with a lawyer called Calatayud. I arrive well combed and very nervous, holding my mother's hand. Already there waiting is my father, looking very serious, and my brother Daniel whose face is buried in a grim silence.

Daniel raises his hand timidly to say hello, while my dad looks at me coldly, no hugs or kisses. Then he just says, "Hello, son."

"Hi dad," I answer, in a low voice.

"I hope you mean it when you call me Dad," he replies.

I don't want to talk to him any more than I have to. It's just that after the abduction, I'm still very hurt by what he did. I suppose that being a father is never easy, but even if mistakes are made, a father should never steal his son away.

After a few customary introductions, I'm left alone in a huge office with the lawyer. He asks me to sit down opposite him in a big chair in front of his old-smelling desk. He explains that he's going to ask me a very simple question and that he wants me to answer him from the heart.

I don't quite understand what that means, 'from the heart', because my heart doesn't exactly have a mouth, but I say nothing. I'm not seeking an explanation because I'm afraid. My mind is troubled by this huge scary office and by virtue of the fact that I'm sat alone with this important man, Calatayud, dressed in a brown three-piece suit, who wants to ask my speechless heart something transcendental.

He opens by saying, "Esteban, you do know that your mum and dad have decided to separate, right?"

"What does it mean to separate?"

"Separation is like divorce. However, the annulment of marriage is forbidden in Argentina and since your parents no longer wish to live together, and divorce doesn't exist, the only option is separation. You already know that, don't you?"

I can't understand a word of this long explanation other than the word *separation*.

"Ah, yes, yes, I know that, sir," I respond shyly, feeling my eyes moisten already; I remember that at school the children of separated parents are looked upon strangely, even badly.

"Well, I have to ask you who you want to live with, your father or your mother?"

"My mother," I answer without hesitating.

"Ok, thank you very much, you can leave now."

When I step out of the office, Calatayud calls in my brother, closing the door behind him. I can't hear what they're talking about, but shortly after, the lawyer calls us all in and says, "Alright then, the children have decided. Daniel is going to live with Pedro and Esteban with Ester.

And that's how I end up staying with my mother for the rest of my early youth; Daniel, on the other hand, lasts only a few weeks with my father. It turns out being a father is too tiresome for Pedro, so first he leaves my brother in an English boarding school and then at grandma Berta's house, with grandpa Pedro Ramón, where he stays forever.

I can't understand that something as important as my parents' separation has just taken place. I soon start to feel their estrangement is because of me, though Mum tries to convince me otherwise by saying that they're adults, independent people with their own problems and desires, and that I'm not to blame for their ultimate goodbye.

I initially feel a great resentment towards my father, because he didn't strive to be with me. I always thought a father would do anything to be with his children, but it seems mine wouldn't. Anyhow, I'm now resigned to having him for a father; that's to say, he can be my father but I'm certainly not his son. I can even feel grateful to life for *not* having a father like him, as this situation has taught me whom I don't want to resemble when I'm older.

Will my father change and try to get closer to me? Can we expect people to change?

CHAPTER NINE
María Belén
Attractive and daring

My brother Daniel is attending the technical school in San Isidro and he tells me how hard it is to study there. He wears a neat uniform comprising grey trousers, sky blue shirt, blue tie and a dark blue blazer. His school supplies are expensive too: a drawing board, a transparent yellow acrylic T-ruler, set squares, protractors, calipers, lead pencils both thick and fine, and rubbers far more efficient than the ones I make out of breadcrumbs. Besides that, he has compasses for geometry, a set of special Rotring pens for technical drawing, and a grey overall for days in the workshop. He also studies German and technical English. He knows a lot. I think he must be a genius.

When I go to visit him at my grandparents' house, I flick through his English books and can hardly understand a thing, but I do recognize some of the words my Aunt Myrtha taught me; when something clicks it makes me hungry to know more. Dani now lives in a spacious apartment at Jacinto Díaz Street in San Isidro.

It's a nice, clean place with all the amenities. It has electricity, a fridge, washing machine, gas stove with oven, lots of decorations and even an electric iron. I'm struck to see photos of my brother and father, which my grandparents have framed. There are none of me. On the wall there's a Magen David on a cross made of lilac-coloured pearls, grandma Berta's favourite colour. She says it represents her bond with my grandfather Pedro.

I wanted to understand and help the ants in my shack to

improve their lot. I collected some black soil and put it into a large rectangular-shaped fish tank, then gradually added a bit of water to harden the soil. With the utmost respect, I invited a queen ant and several other ant families to make the fish tank their home; for weeks I fed them leaves, fodder and breadcrumbs, coaxing them not to give up their work. I spent hours talking to the ants earnestly in this way. It didn't take long for them to get organised and dig several tunnels, thereby erecting a beautiful anthill with secret passageways and galleries where they stored seeds. Back on the surface I scattered little cotton flakes and kept them moist so that the ants always had water too.

Through the glass walls of the fish tank, which was tightly closed above with a piece of fine wire mesh, bit by bit I followed their arduous work of building a beautiful anthill with both delight and admiration; it looked like a five-star hotel that housed a colony of about two hundred ants. Before setting them free I wanted to share their labour of love with my brother. Warm with enthusiasm, I therefore brought the fish tank to my grandparents' house thinking they'd be fascinated by such beauty; alas, they showed no interest whatsoever in my little friends, the ants. I left them in the covered patio and went to take a shower. When I returned, I found them all dead. Grandma Berta had decided to spray them all with Raid, an insecticide.

My brother, on the other hand, is very kind. He loves me and treats me well; he gives me the clothes he doesn't wear, shows me the blueprints he makes and the things he builds at school.

He goes out running and to do physical exercise every afternoon, in Plaza Don Bosco. He sometimes invites me along, but I can't compete with him. He beats me at everything. I visit him from time to time but not as much as I'd like.

I sense that my presence there is not very welcome. When I do go I try at least to take a shower with their wonderful hot water. It never ceases to amaze me how they have a bathtub and taps with flowing water. I take forever in the bathroom, not only creating self-absorbed onanistic images under this delightful warm rain, but also actually washing my body, and then applying copious amounts of Grandma's special *Sapolán Ferrini* cream to every inch of my skin. I always look forward to a shower, the moment I can remove the accumulated crust of grime from my body. I love the hot water, the *Sedal* shampoo, and the *Heno de Pravia* green soap, with its fine aroma of herbs and flowers, which I know are always waiting for me.

Grandma Berta doesn't like the fact that my showers are so long. She tells me that I shouldn't use up so much water and that it's much better for me to have a quick wash. She also supervises the amount of loo paper I use. She wants to know how exactly I use it and even asks me to show her. She follows me into the bathroom and then I act out the scenario, watching as her soft face, so pure and white, hardens into an expression of disbelief tempered with anger. She frowns and without holding back asks me, "Who taught you to make the paper into a bun before cleaning your bottom?" Grandma is much too refined to say *bum*. I explain that this is just how I do it at my mum's house.

I'm reluctant to tell her that we use newspaper to wipe our bums at home, and that Mum taught me that by scrunching it into a small bun and then opening it back up, the paper is softer and doesn't scratch so much.

I love my Lala, I really do, but she sometimes does things that I don't understand and that put in doubt the love between us. For example, she won't let me sleep in my brother's bedroom. When I occasionally stay the night she makes me sleep on a red sofa in the living room; it's rather uncomfortable but at least my legs fit in there okay. I lie down and think about why things are this way. Since I can't find an answer I start counting, sometimes for hours on end to see how high I can go. Today I reached 5708 before I finally fell asleep.

When grandma Berta serves us at the table, she always gives Daniel more food. There's no fresh orange juice for me either; she says my brother needs more vitamin C and she also gives him another vitamin called B12. On top of that, whenever she offers us Coca-Cola, she always adds a splash of water to my glass. She seems to have so many little rules and is just steeped in her own biases. The injustice does upset me somewhat but I learn that the only way to free myself from this negative feeling is not to hate my grandmother or be jealous of the preferential treatment she gives my brother; I can make it all disappear by extinguishing any desire I may have for orange juice, squeezed by her delicate hands, unadulterated Coca-Cola or the B12 supplement. In effect, I do just that: I eliminate the desire, accept reality as it is, and I manage to put an end to my suffering.

I'm not sure what to continue studying now. I'm about to finish Year 8 at my school, Sargento Mayor Bernabé Márquez, known for short as Escuela No. 6. There are some days I dream of being a firefighter, others a pediatrician, and sometimes even a teacher or journalist. But now the time to decide has come and I've no idea which secondary school I want to attend.

If I go to the Commercial School in San Isidro, I'll end up having to study lots of maths and accountancy, two subjects that I do like but that aren't my passion. My brother Daniel suggests I join him in the industrial school.

I take his advice and for several weeks leading up to the entrance exam I work away alone at maths, Spanish language and general culture knowledge. I pass my exams at the first attempt, and I'm in! It's as if, unintentionally, overnight, I turn into another Daniel. I like the idea too because I really look up to him.

My brother hands me down almost all the components of my new uniform: a pair of grey trousers now too small for him, a blue shirt he no longer wears, a tie, a metal school badge, and a dark blue blazer with beautiful patches sewn onto the elbows by grandma Berta with her new Singer sewing machine.

The black shoes I provide myself, because I found them one afternoon sifting through a rubbish bin in the affluent neighbourhood along Calle Diego Palma, just before the corner of Segundo Fernández. To some extent I feel fortunate that my brain is now so used to recycling things others throw away, things that can still be of use to me. This pair of shoes are certainly worn out, with holes in their soles, but after a good polish they look great; it's only on rainy days that my feet get a bit wet, but I can solve that problem by stuffing newspaper inside them.

In no way do I dislike finding discarded things and using them, but I do often dream of being able to buy brand new clothes, especially a pair of shoes. I'd really love to own shoes of my own, be the only one who's set foot inside them.

Getting to the technical school is fairly exhausting in itself. I get up at six o'clock in the morning, eat a piece of bread, have a cup of black tea, and then walk seven blocks to Avenida Márquez, on the corner of Blanco Encalada, from where I hitch a ride to Avenida Centenario and then cover the last stretch on foot. Sometimes I'm lucky and get picked up by the Military Mayor of San Isidro, Don José María Noguer.

The mayor doesn't talk to me about anything while he

drives along, but he leaves me just two blocks from school and for that I'm grateful. He seems just like Sosa, another military man who's head of the workshop at school, a very serious man who inspires plenty of fear in all of us. You see, the military now hold command posts everywhere. This satrap, for example, forces us to go to school with our hair super short, almost shaved; it's not allowed to interfere with the shirt collar.

We're also forbidden to smoke within a perimeter of five blocks around the school, nor can we go to the cinema opposite the municipal building where they show films starring Isabel Sarli, an actress very much in vogue, whose breasts are even bigger than those of María Belén...

María Belén is a girl at my new school, ENETSI (Escuela Nacional de Educación Técnica of San Isidro); it's mainly for boys, I guess, but there are two other determined girls who also opted for industrial education.

On the whole, I have a pretty good time at this school, and even get to have fun sometimes, but it's very demanding; you have to study all the time and there's always lots of homework to be done. I also have to take lunch with me for the two days we spend in the workshop every week, which means finding food we don't actually have at home. On top of that, everything about me is meant to be spotless; and yet, we don't even have a washing machine at home, let alone a clean table where I can do homework. It would be fair to say that it entails a good deal of sacrifice all round. I just don't think I can take the pace of it much longer. I think studying beyond elementary school isn't quite right for me. What choice do I really have? Perhaps the best thing I can do is dedicate myself to finding a job and abandon my desire to learn altogether.

I consider all my classmates to be good friends because I don't have a problem with any of them, but the guys I most like hanging out with and chatting to are Russo, Belsito, Ansaldo, Alderete, Rossi, Mantoán, Cruz, Doval, Fiore, Sardi, Di Martino, Trusso and Di Tomaso. Almost all of them are of Italian stock, and warm in character too, just like part of me.

The subjects I enjoy most here are Spanish language and literature, geography and everything we do in the workshop. In carpentry, I make a four-legged bench starting from scratch with a square board. I take the measurements, make the necessary cuts and holes, sand the different bits down and glue them together producing a marvelous piece of furniture and a 10/10 score for my final grade.

In tinwork, I make a small jug out of an old can of cooking oil, just like the ones covering the exterior walls of my little shanty home. I open the cans up, flatten them, take the measurements, make the cuts, weld the bits together, along with a handle and a neck, and *voilà!* a fine addition to our kitchen cupboards, and another good mark…

In ironwork, I make a near-perfect hammer starting out

with a chunk of raw iron. I first shape it in the lathe machine, and then finish it off with a file, counting on my hands alone for precision. I also make an iron trivet (the welds look seamless!) and offer it to my mum as a gift; she doesn't have an iron yet, but one day I'll get her one.

Finally, in electrics, I make an electrical circuit board. Everything works out fine and I get more good grades, but the materials are expensive, really expensive, including the books, and Mum has to make a huge sacrifice for me.

She sacrifices her own dreams so that I myself can dream of completing secondary school.

Some of my teachers really are outstanding: Sra. Benatar in history, Sra. Casan in mathematics; but, in geography, I have the best teacher in the whole school, Don Eduardo Sciosi. He's a devout Christian and walks with a limp, due to contracting polio as a child; one of his shoe soles is about 20 centimetres high so that it can match the length of his other leg. He's never visited any other country outside of Argentina, but in his master classes he takes us all over the world with him.

He teaches us that in order for a person to feel complete in their life they must visit and, if possible, live in the land of their ancestors. He talks about the importance of knowing the different languages that run through our veins. During his classes I promise to one day visit, live and study the languages of Israel, Italy and Germany. As soon as I'm able to, I'll go, I promise myself.

It is thanks to these geography classes that, without ever having left Argentina either, I already feel like I know the whole world and I'm fascinated by how wondrous it seems. I want to go everywhere, starting with Israel.

Today he whisks us off to China, telling us that very strange and interesting things happen there every day. He says, for example, that it has a rich culture and that, despite being an extremely poor country in which every bug that walks, flies, swims or crawls ends up on the grill, it has much to offer. That sounds disgusting, I know, but he goes on to say that China has an ancient history, beautiful paintings, imposing architecture and delicious food.

I can't imagine what Chinese food looks and tastes like (apart from the insects of course, and even that's quite hard!) and I've never seen a Chinese man, let alone a restaurant serving Chinese food. He tells us that its capital is called Beijing and that the rest of the vast country is rather quiet; that communism governs the nation with an iron fist, and that consequently the country is very safe for foreigners.

He says that it's almost impossible for someone there to cheat you, attack you or steal from you; that the Chinese are good people who move about the place on millions of bicycles and who treat all foreigners as welcome guests; that because they're not allowed to complain, they work *like the Chinese*, that's to say, very hard; that soon they're going to get ahead and become a great world power.

They have a gigantic, geographically diverse country with almost eight hundred million inhabitants, the most populous nation on the planet, and Sr. Sciosi regrets that almost no one is baptised because the prevailing religion is something called *Confucianism*, which fosters discipline and honesty.

Sr. Sciosi then explains to us that because the population is so big, the government forbids couples having more than one child; if a woman doesn't take care of herself and falls pregnant with a second child, she's obliged to have an abortion. It's very sad.

He also mentions that Chinese calligraphy is a true art and that many languages are spoken across the country; the main ones are Mandarin and Cantonese.

He tells us that the Great Wall of China can be seen from the low Earth orbit, and that Hong Kong, which is now a British enclave, ought to once again return to China, just as the Falkland Islands should to Argentina. Our charismatic and knowledgeable teacher ends the lesson talking about Taiwan, saying that it's an island populated by more Chinese people who are not communist, but democratic and capitalist. He continues to prophesy that surely one day, not too far away, that island will once again be an integral part of the great Chinese nation and that, just as now, the common people believe that sushi is of Japanese origin or that pasta is of Italian origin and not

Chinese, that in just a few more decades the Chinese will *chinatize* the whole world without us realizing it.

I myself prophesy that one day, not too far away, I'll visit the lands of the Chinese and eat their strange food, with or without chopsticks, and walk along their imposing wall.

At the start of the school year, they had us make a list of our personal details—name, address and phone number—to facilitate communication between students, which is especially useful for when we're later divided into groups of three and given practical work. I wrote down my address, Acceso Norte Street, Lomas de San Isidro, and then the phone number for grandma Berta's house, 743-3527.

A few weeks pass and then one afternoon around six o'clock, I'm in my house, playing with Lulu, when suddenly I hear someone calling at the door, knocking quite loudly, clapping their hands. I open up and there before me are two boys from school, the redhead Doval and the good-natured Trusso. As soon as I recognise them I blush with shame and they in turn frown at me with surprise. I can't believe they've come to visit me without any warning. They must've found my address on the students' list!

"Is this where you really live, Esteban?" They ask me, almost simultaneously.

We look at each other in silence. I can feel one of those knots curling and twisting in my throat like a snake; I'm unable to utter a single word to them and I think they quickly realise the unintentional humiliation they've caused me with their unexpected visit for they soon leave without saying any more.

I never want to go back to that school again. How will I ever be able to look them in the face?
It's been five days in a row now that I've skived off. Mum is so worried that she asks Aunt Myrtha for some help; she in turn offers to look after me at her house the next time I go in to the workshop, feeding me and washing my clothes too. Another day in the week I can go to grandma Berta's house but she still asks Mum to bring some food with her as she already has enough expenses with my brother Daniel.

Mum eventually convinces me to go back to school and I do so against my better judgement, still consumed by a deep fear. When I step into the classroom, everyone unsurprisingly looks around at me. My heart sinks as I realise that my former friends, now potential tormentors, Doval and Trusso, have told the rest of the class about 'the dismal conditions in which Esteban lives…' The response to this, however, is far more positive than I could ever have imagined; there's no callous smirking or whispers, just expressions of candid concern. I'm quickly adopted back into the classroom family as if it were nothing and soon other kids are inviting me for sandwiches and fruit during breaktime and to their homes too. Things have never been better. On top of that, I've been given a new nickname: *Ciche*, the class mascot.

I have many vivid memories from these days at school. I remember one time when a much-loved man died in San Isidro, a member of an influential family by the name of Béccar Varela. I don't know which one he was, but I'm quite sure he was the eldest; usually it's that way, the elder ones dying first.

The wake is taking place in the municipal building right across from school and the headmaster, Sr. Tolosa, enters our classroom announcing that we'll be the ones charged with taking turns to hold vigil for the deceased. He explains that we have to stand up straight with our eyes cast slightly downwards and our bodies stock still, two at a time, one on either side of the coffin.

I pair up with a kid called Hernández who's the same height as me. The glossy mahogany coffin is wide open, the dead man in it finely attired, shaved, scented and lightly powdered. He certainly doesn't smell like a dead man; in fact, he looks like a living person who's simply asleep. An endless parade of people files into the room to pay their last respects; some even shed a few tears in front of old Don Béccar Varela. This is the first time I've attended a funeral, for when grandma Raquel died, I wasn't invited to her final farewell.

Secondary school quickly becomes the central interest in my life as a teenager. Being separated from my illustrious father quite early on, and having grown up with a mother who also plays the role of a father, who's always busy working at the hospital or cleaning at home or just sleeping due to exhaustion, I feel that I lack many of the experiences other kids have had, which is why I need school more than they do.

I need to be constantly reading books and newspapers to catch up a bit. I'd have loved to have a father to guide me at times, to have learnt from him and with him, but since I don't, I feel I must stay all the more alert, pay greater attention to my surroundings so that I can gain the necessary experience and insight to face life and be able to keep up with the other kids my age, kids who have both their parents around and seemingly almost everything in life.

I haven't seen my father in years now, I know he's been living in Córdoba again, now with his fourth wife, but ever since he gave up all parental custody of me, our contact ended. He doesn't visit me anymore, he doesn't reply to my letters and he doesn't even leave me a greeting on the phone at grandma Berta's house anymore. It's all very disheartening; a total rejection that's likely the reason I've stopped talking about my father altogether. It's over.

How do you forget someone you love? Can you really forget a child?

CHAPTER TEN
Gabriela

My mother now needs my help more than ever, especially after the birth of my new brother, Marcos David. When her maternity leave finishes, I'm in charge of taking care of him, preparing his bottle, changing his diapers and washing them by hand.

After two years, our life is further complicated when my little brother contracts meningitis. He spends weeks in the children's hospital on the brink of death. Though he eventually makes a recovery, he now needs even more attention. When he returns home, he has to relearn how to walk and be a normal child again.

It becomes necessary that I leave school to get a full-time job, to be independent, so that I can provide an extra income to help my mother with the added expenses at home.

During my free time I wander over the land bordering the Pan-American Highway where people throw away garbage to look for anything of use. I collect bits of wire that I then melt down to get copper and sell by weight.

Lately, there seem to be many cables lying about as they're putting up electric lanterns to illuminate the streets. There are always loose pieces left behind by employees of Segba, the Electricity Service of Greater Buenos Aires.

Bronze pays well, but it's harder to find; aluminum a bit

less, as it's a staple in most rubbish bins. Besides that, I pick up old tea pots, broken casseroles, buckets and various other cooking utensils that the rich are fast replacing with plastic ones.

This is becoming more apparent now that the ladies of the Lomas de San Isidro, when gathered in their houses for tea, are beginning to speak of these curious containers called Tupperware. Apparently they're used for storing food. But they are something new only be found at get-togethers organised by high-society women. It must be why I'm currently finding more and more aluminium containers in the rubbish.

Another well-rewarded but rather work-intensive endeavour is the collection of aluminium wrapping from cigarette packets. It's hard to get my hands on because you have to rustle the rubbish about a fair bit for the packets to appear, grab them, and then separate the aluminium from the common paper so it can be sold in stacks like banknotes. With the money I make selling these precious materials, I'm able to help my mother and keep some of it to pay for my bus tickets and buy a newspaper every day.

I now have the habit of reading the paper six days a week: I like to buy La Nación because of its size, I have to open my arms wide to read it. There's another new daily called El Pregón which I also quite like as it claims to break down the news in a more digestible way. I collect almost all of their issues and the smell of freshly-printed ink makes it all the more pleasant to read.

I read them from cover to cover, just like Mirtha Legrand, usually while travelling on the bus. Once I finish with them I take them home where they are used to make fires, clean surfaces, soak the oil from the frying pan, and even as a tablecloth or napkins.

They also serve to plug the holes in the roof of our shack and prevent the cold from entering between the grooves in the wood, layering them thickly over the walls.

It is often the case that older people interrupt me when I'm reading the newspaper on the bus or train to congratulate me.

-Very good boy, you read the paper! It's really quite common, actually. And then there are those who don't dare to talk to me and just sit there looking at me curiously, while others simply smile. I can't understand why it's so special for them to see a child reading the newspaper on public transport. What else is there to do?

Today, after waking with my mother at dawn, I leave the house early and, this time, pick out an issue of Clarín from the news-stand. It's a little more expensive than El Pregón, but more useful too. Scanning through the jobs section, I see an advert seeking an office boy for a dental lab called Rotadent. It's located in the capital district; I go for a job interview and am taken on instantly, and asked to distribute dentures throughout the city of Buenos Aires.

I perform this menial job with great commitment, passion and dedication—although working as an office boy in a dental laboratory, walking around all day with the smell of monomer stuck to my clothes, might not seem all that amusing to most people.

My colleagues working in the lab are very kind people and from day one they've shown me a lot of patience. Especially Jorge, who writes a long list of directions every day for me detailing how to get to each of the dental practices awaiting dentures, single teeth, crowns and bridges.

The note might explain to me, for example, how to take the metro line "D" towards Catedral, get off on 9 de Julio station and change for line "C" towards Plaza Constitución, then get off at Avenida de Mayo station, change there for line "A", head to Primera Junta and finally get off at Plaza Miserere station.

Jorge often goes further, "Esteban, you have to take line "A" which is the one built by the British in 1913, so the direction of the trains goes the same way it does in England: from the left."

I really like this line because the wagons have wooden interiors, even the seats. Plus, each of the stations has a different tile colour. When they built the line very few people could read, so they'd say: get off at the green station, or the brown. Jorge's instructions are extremely valuable to me allowing me to really get to know the City. It's not long before I become a 'professional' office boy.

One of my favourite resting places in the centre of Buenos

Aires is the historic Plaza de Mayo; there is always a loftier energy emanating from the thousands of people and pigeons that pass by there daily.

I often pause my work to listen to Don Duarte, an old man who is usually to be found in the Metropolitan Cathedral explaining very interesting things about the Mausoleum of General San Martín. From him I learn that the Father of the Fatherland was embalmed, and that owing to miscalculations he rests in the mausoleum today at a 45 degree angle. So he's almost been seated for over a hundred years.

Today I'm going to see Don Duarte again, but I can't find him. The mausoleum is closed to the public because they're doing repair work. I sneak in anyway and talk to the chief archaeologist in charge of the work. Her name is Rita. I introduce myself explaining that I am a disciple of Don Duarte. She smiles at me and greets me warmly saying that Don Duarte had indeed told her of my existence. This use of the word 'existence' is strange to me, but true.

My arrival coincides with the opening of the coffin of Tomás Guido, another Argentine military, diplomat, politician and friend of General San Martín.

I immediately sense that Rita likes me, but it still comes as a surprise when she invites me in to help her clean the bones of Don Guido, who died in 1866.

Even more surprising is that the bones are rather dry and odourless. Copying Rita, I pick them up them one by one, with great respect for the deceased, clean them very carefully with a brush, removing the dust, and place them on a table. Once that task is completed, one by one we return them to his coffin.

On my return to the lab, I excitedly tell Gimeno, one of the dental technicians, who is also from Córdoba like me, "I just had Tomás Guido in my hands…"
"Stop talking nonsense, Esteban," he replies and goes back to his work polishing a few false teeth.
So I keep quiet, preferring not to explain anything more to anyone. It may be difficult for others to understand that I have just shaken hands with someone who died more than a hundred years ago.

After a few months shuttling hundreds of teeth around the city, I sit down with the owner of the dental lab and explain to him that I urgently need some more money; my sister Claudia Naomi has just been born and the expenses at home have once again increased. He tells me he's very happy with me, but he can't raise my salary. He can, however, offer me an extra day off every week, so that I can go out and look for another job to supplement my pay. I accept, and choose Mondays; there are hardly any teeth to deliver on this day.
"Hopefully you can find another job that allows you to study, Esteban. I can see you're ready for more."

The very next Monday I get up early with my mother, at four-thirty in the morning. She starts work at six, as a maid at the San Isidro Public Health Care clinic. I'm on the lookout for a new job. She prepares me a cup of boiled *mate-tea* along with a piece of hard bread, just as I like it, and gives me her blessing, putting her hands on my head, looking me in the eye and reciting the prayer, "May God bless you and keep you, may His face shine upon you and be gracious to you; may He lift up His countenance upon you and give you peace." Then she kisses me and turns towards the door, but not before offering one last piece of advice, "Think well, my dear boy, and everything will turn out just fine."

"Yes, Mama, thank you," I reply.

I head out a short while later. I take the 333 bus and arrive at San Isidro station around seven. I walk up to the ticket office and buy a return ticket to the city centre, far cheaper than the cost of two individual trips.

The ticket itself looks unduly important for such a short trip, it's only an hour long. It measures about four centimetres by two, is made of hard cardboard, and is marked on either side by a different colour: a white side to be punched out on the first trip and an orange side designated for the return.

The guard is dressed in grey, with a cap, jacket and tie. There is a whistle hanging from his neck and a metal ticket punch in his hand.

I buy a copy of the Clarín newspaper from the kiosk on the Mitre railway line platform. A train to Retiro comes along and I hop on. The seats on this line are upholstered in green; their backs can be turned up either way to suit the direction of travel. One can't always decide but I prefer to sit in the same direction as the train is going. Finding an empty double seat, I sit down, open the paper and hastily flick to the classified jobs section where I start marking in blue all the ads offering office boy positions whose addresses I plan to visit in my morning's quest.

I mark with a tick a fair number of other job notices of all kinds; the good thing is that I have a lot to aim at. They're looking for office boys, salesmen, shop assistants, menial workers and clerks. Countless vendors file up and down the train selling needle threaders, sweets, scarves made of monkey hair, and all the national newspapers: Crónica, Clarín, La Nación, Tiempo Argentino, La Razón, El Pregón, and Ambito Financiero. Some hand out stamps of saints and virgins, while others beg or busk. Misery and entertainment are a carriage apart, but I let nothing distract me from my goal. I must find work today.

At the station of Martinez something does catch my gaze: a man boards the train, immaculately dressed with a beautiful tie around his neck, and sits himself right next to me.

He must be about forty years old. I take quick stock of his short black hair, his neatness in every regard, his discreet scent, and finally notice him glancing furtively down at my newspaper. He is watching what I'm doing, following the movements of my pen as it shifts along the rows upon rows of offers. His attitude is beginning to unnerve me, slowly filling me with animosity.

I consider it a blatant invasion of my privacy, and so to

deter his curiosity I slightly tilt my body towards him, using my torso to somewhat block his intrusive view.

I continue in this way, absorbed in my earnest selection, until the train comes to a halt at Rivadavia Station. Here, after the guard passes by punching our tickets, the suited man looks directly at me and asks, "Looking for a job?"
I pretend, churlishly, that I haven't heard the question.
"I can give you a job," he tells me.
"Thank you, sir, but there's no need for that. I'll find another job today," I reply without looking at him.

After another twenty minutes sitting next to this gentleman, who seems so good-natured, but who out of pride I prefer to ignore, my mother's words come back to me: "Think well and everything will turn out just fine." But I still dare not talk to the man. I feel that the peace my mother bestowed on me in her morning blessing left my body a while ago.
More and more discomfort seems to be arising from this unexpected situation.

The train makes its usual restrained entrance at Retiro Central Station, at which point my stubbornly curious travel companion pulls out a card from the top pocket of his impeccable blue suit and hands it to me saying, "If you don't find a job, come and see me."
"I don't plan on seeing you, sir, because I'm going to find another job. But thank you anyway," I reply very dryly, slipping the card into one of my pockets.

From the station I begin my fruitless search. I take the underground line "C" towards Constitución and get off at Diagonal Norte, deciding to go on foot from there. I visit two Japanese-run dry cleaners, a pharmacy, a warehouse, two greengrocers, and several other offices scattered about the area. I'm told everywhere more or less the same thing, "We're looking for someone over the age of eighteen, who has either completed their military service or is exempt from it.

So off I trot to try my luck at a pizzeria called Las Cuartetas on Avenida Corrientes. I notice the owner is a Spaniard, like almost everyone who has a pizzeria in Buenos Aires. He listens to my plea in a congenial manner and then, without a hint of compassion, tells me, "Look lad, you don't quite look mature enough to work here. I'm looking for someone eighteen and up, someone with a little more experience. And muscle, for that matter."

"That's tough to know for sure at first glance, sir. You yourself look *mature* but not exactly strong. Anyway, mister, I bet all those over eighteens you want will only arrive late to work, they'll be taking days off pretending to be sick and they'll never be as responsible as I am—your loss."

"Have you looked at yourself in the mirror lately?" he retorts, "You're too young and frail. Go eat some more, grow up a bit, and then you can come back."

After breathing in the delectable smell of freshly baked pizza and *fainá* emanating from every corner of Las Cuartetas, I let out a long sigh and lumber off, even hungrier and angrier than when I went in. How could I not persuade this silly Spaniard who was so quick to say what he thought?

Thirst can be readily quenched anywhere with water, but the pains of hunger have deeper roots and are not so easy to relieve. Hunger mixed with anger is even worse.

It's true that I'm a bit short in stature, and quite skinny too, but I'm switched on and I have all the experience I need. At least, as an office boy. Plus, I know my way around Buenos Aires pretty well now. And I've worked from the age of nine in the warehouses of Lolita and Elvira, in a shanty town called Villa La Cava, so I know what good service is all about, how to clean up and be friendly to customers. What does he know about it?

After a lot of walking, my feet are now aching considerably. I still have two more places to check from the twelve that I marked in the newspaper, but they're quite far away, one in Caballito and the other by the cemetery in Chacarita.

I pause to think. It's already three o'clock in the afternoon and I haven't had any lunch. I'm hungry and exhausted. I dig into my pocket and take out my National Identity Card and a folded green banknote of fifty thousand pesos, enough to buy a sandwich and a soft drink. But there in between them, glinting at me, is the business card given to me by the man in the nice blue suit from the train. On it is written:

Germán González Chiappe
Festo Pneumatic
Director
1235 Avenida Belgrano
Capital Federal, Argentina

When recalling the physical appearance of the man, a certain TV journalist comes to mind who hosts a night show once a week. I think his name is Grondona, yes that's it, he looks just like Mariano Grondona, a great journalist, incidentally.

I resolve to go to his office, setting off from the Obelisk, it's neither close nor far. When I arrive at the building, I find the company on the ground floor. A secretary receives me at the door and I request to speak to the director, proudly presenting her the card he gave me just before getting off the train.

She then leaves for a few minutes. I look beyond the high counter at reception to find a number of desks arranged in rows, each strewn with papers, occupied by someone talking on the phone, drawing blueprints or writing. I notice that some of the employees, almost entirely men, look over at me curiously. At length, the secretary returns and introduces herself saying, "I'm Gabriela, Gabriela Oliva. The director will see you now."

Gabriela is a very slight and elegant young woman, with short black hair and beautiful skin. She's also tall and has a very delicate demeanour. She leads me through a long corridor of desks until we come to an office with wooden frames and big glass windows. It looks to me like a huge fish tank which has only one fish inside, the biggest of them all.

Here he is, the director, this Mariano Grondona lookalike, the honest-faced and well-dressed businessman from the train, now without his blue jacket, the sleeves of his bright white shirt neatly rolled up. I can hear him talking on the phone in German and when he sees me he gestures at me to come in and sit down. As I enter he continues talking and goes to fish something out of his blue jacket which is hanging on a coat stand at the end of his long wooden desk. The long black cable fixed to the dial is at full stretch, slowly coiling back up as he returns to the centre of the desk with his wallet. He then shakes my hand without addressing me, talking all the while, and I look at him starting to feel a little nervous but trying not to show it. The whole situation is very new and bizarre for me.

He finally opens up his wallet, pulls out a reddish million-peso note and, without hanging up the phone, says to me, "Please go and find me some change for this, there are lots of shops on the block." He hands over the banknote, incidentally the largest we currently have in circulation, in the same manner he gave me his card, and returns his attention once again to the phone conversation in German. I'm totally shocked by the request but, not wanting to further interrupt him, I turn and leave.

Stepping out of the building, first I go to a pharmacy where they tell me they're all out of small bills. Next I try the bakery on the corner where the smell of freshly baked bread cruelly reawakens my hunger, making my guts squeal in their plea for nourishment. But here too I seem out of luck as the owner grunts, also in a thick Iberian accent, "We don't give out change here. This is not a bank, it is a bakery."

"But the change is for the director of Festo Pneumatic," I reply, "I'm the new office boy there and we really need the change. Please help me, sir."

A look of surprise spreads across his face and without saying another word he gives me ten beige coloured notes, one hundred thousand pesos each.

I've no idea if this engineer, Chiappe, will give me a job, but after my first impressions of his company, I'm already looking forward to it, even if its name does make me think of pasta with pesto.

I return at once to the fish tank office and, after knocking cautiously on the door, I enter handing out the million pesos to the director. Without even counting, he puts the money away in a drawer of his desk and then turns to me, "So, what's your name?"

"Esteban."

"How old are you?"

"Fourteen and three quarters."

He smiles. "Are you studying?"

"No, I dropped out of my technical school in December, after completing two years there, but I want to finish high school as soon as possible.

"Where did you go looking for change?"

"First I went to the pharmacy—no luck—then I went to the bakery where the Spanish cashier didn't want to give me change either, but I told him that the change was for you and that I'm the new office boy in Festo Pneumatic."

He smiles again and says, "Esteban, welcome to our company! You will take your instructions from Gabriela, my secretary. You need only work the number of hours you're comfortable with daily, so that you can continue studying, and remember you must always be punctual and never lie.

"Thank you, sir, and please forgive the discourtesy I showed you on the train."

"That was nothing."

So begins the best job in my life. I soon find out Germán González Chiappe is an Argentine engineer, founder and director of the new German automation company Festo Pneumatic in Argentina. I mean, it's a new established multinational. Gabriela immediately sets about introducing me to each of the employees as the head office boy of the company. In actual fact, I'm the only office boy, but that doesn't take the shine off my appointment.

On the train ride home, I remember the blessing my mother gave me that very morning. I recall her advice to think positively and reflect on the miracle I have experienced today. I realise everything that happens around me never ceases to amaze me. I'm filled with happiness and begin to wonder what miracles mean for me. Do miracles really exist? And what are they?

CHAPTER ELEVEN
Hebe
Suffered and mutant

Here at Festo Pneumatic, everyone's treating me really well and I'm learning so much about the importance of order, good manners, discipline, keeping to schedules and working as a team. The team of engineers is led by a man called Bronzini, who's constantly boasting of there being order in amongst the clutter of his desk; then there are the secretaries, the technicians, those who work in storage and cleaning, and, of course, me, the head (and only!) office boy.

We all eat together in the building, with tasty dishes served up by Eustakia, our talented and friendly Paraguayan cook, and it's as if we're a big family, sat at the long table next to the kitchen, right behind the fish-tank office.

I'm getting paid pretty well now and I can help out my mum a lot more at home, buying milk powder for my little sister Claudia Naomi and supplies for my little brother Marcos David who's already started primary school.

The company director, Germán González Chiappe, has also become something of a teacher to me. He can speak Spanish, German, English and French all fluently, and I love languages too; he teaches me to see them as useful tools which can open doors to new worlds, "especially if one learns how to say 'pull' and 'push'", he says jokingly.

I want to master several foreign languages; in fact, it's been my intention for a long time now. I guess it all began back when I use to collect old bits of cable down by Pan-American Highway; I would melt them down and then sell the copper by the gram. In this way I managed to save up enough money to buy an Aristos Spanish-English dictionary. Ever since, I've tried to learn one new word a day in English. The other languages I'll leave for later; slowly but surely I know I'll pick them all up.

Gabriela Oliva, the company secretary, is studying German at the Goethe Institute on Avenida Corrientes. I'd love to go there myself, but the Goethe is as good as it is expensive.

I now have an agreement with the director and Gabriela: every time Sr. Chiappe is on the phone to the headquarters in Esslingen, Germany, Gabriela has to warn me so that I can leave what I'm doing and go to the fish-tank door to listen in on the conversation.

When the director sees me, he gives me a smile, knowing how much I love listening to the strange words he's speaking. He also teaches me the odd thing. At lunchtime one day, he turns to me saying, *"Esteban, ich habe hunger. Bist du hungrig auch?"*

"Ja, herr Direktor, ich bin hungrig zu", I respond.

There's a man in storage called Natalio; he speaks in a very slow and measured way and has been at Festo since the formation of the company. Like Gabriela, he teaches me many things, mostly to do with hydraulics: how it works, the names and functions of spare parts, threads, compressors, valves, filters, pumps, cylinders, flanges, couplers, and hundreds of other little items that come numbered and packaged all the way from Germany. Edgardo explains to me, "The Germans still keep up their custom of numbering everything". I look him in the eye and frown, expressing my disapproval for his dark sense of humour.

When I started the job I committed myself to my boss, promising to finish high school. I have to fulfil that promise but at the same time I can't exactly stop working either; it would be catastrophic for all of us at home if I do. The solution is to attend evening classes.

I sign up to the Escuela Nocturna Juan José Paso on Calle Valentín Gómez 3163, in the central *barrio* of Balvanera-Once, for a course specialising in Literature. It's a boys-only school and most of us are very enthusiastic to be there. We have an excellent team of teachers too, and I soon discover, to my surprise, that I really enjoy going to evening classes.
I work from 9 a.m. to 6 p.m. and then I head to school from 7 p.m. to 10:30 p.m. I never miss a lesson and quickly work out the best route home. From the Jean Jaurés underground station, I take line B to Callao, and from there I take bus number 60, with the *Panamericana* sign on the front, getting back home a little after midnight.

I only get to sleep six hours a night, but it's more than the four hours that the TV host Bernardo Neustadt says he sleeps, and he's much older than me and probably needs more rest too!

Festo Pneumatic is growing very fast and very big, and I'm

growing with it. It's just that because of its ever-expanding size they're going to have to move to a much larger and more comfortable building on Avenida General Paz. Soon I'll be forced to choose between school and work.

After a few months I'm rather fed up with this fast pace of life. Recieving a good formal education is proving increasingly difficult for me due to the growing time pressures. I feel that my level of education is lacking like that of most kids my age who grow up poor and have to work alongside their studies. Deep down, I know I shouldn't really be complaining about it because there are others who are even worse off than me. In Villa La Cava, the shantytown not far from my house, I do volunteering on Sundays, teaching adult immigrants to read and write, and also children who are suffering from serious malnutrition.
I can count myself lucky to have found work. Most of my friends are looking for a job and can't find one. The over 30s either have precarious work or are just unemployed, while the over 50s find it practically impossible to get a job. Those retired like my grandpa Pedro are on a meagre pension and the Junta says that despite these problems, the rest of the population is living the good life. But, what other people are they talking about? I ask myself.

This dictatorship is an absolute disaster so I've decided to respond to the appeal from Saul Ubaldini, leader of the CGT, Confederación General del Trabajo, and, today on 30th March 1982, I'm going to a demonstration in Plaza de Mayo to tell the military to put an end to the starvation of the people. I arrive in *Capital Federal* to find the downtown area has been completely surrounded by repressive forces. None of the varying columns of workers can seem to get even get near Plaza de Mayo. There's a lot of tension in the air, and then we start singing:

"Milicos, muy mal paridos,
Qué es lo que han hecho con los desaparecidos,
La deuda externa, la corrupción?
Son la peor mierda que ha tenido la Nación!"

Translated it goes something like this:

"Milicos, you bunch of demons,
What have you done with all the missing people?
With the external debt, the corruption?
You're the worst shit that ever befell the nation"

This provokes a furious backlash from the *milicos* and they begin to beat everyone back with sticks and fire canisters of teargas, stinging our eyes and noses with unbearable itchiness. In spite of this, thousands of us manage to break through to Plaza de Mayo, withstanding the rubber bullets, the hydrant trucks and even charging horses, mounted by far more beastly animals who are dealing out savage blows with their batons all around us. We use words as our defence, trying to persuade the soldiers and policemen not to obey their orders to beat us. I can see some of them starting to cry, paralysed and unsure how to respond; they don't know whether to follow their orders or hold back and do what's right.

Some of the *milicos* attack us all the more fiercely and we have to fling their gifts of teargas back at them. Demonstrations and chaos of this sort are replicated in other cities across the country. In the end, exhausted from all the fighting, we're forced to make our retreat, arriving home heartbroken and battered.

The de facto president, General Leopoldo Fortunato Galtieri, sober for a change, makes an announcement on television, with no allusion to the ongoing popular protests, of course. Instead, he says that something important is about to happen in Argentina, a vague declaration that arouses the bewilderment and curiosity of all.

Public anguish doesn't last long for on the 2nd April we wake up to the news that the military has recaptured *Las Malvinas,* the Falklands archipelago that until then had been in the hands of the British. That same afternoon, thousands of Argentines once again flock to Plaza de Mayo, this time to celebrate the Argentine victory. This huge historic square is now filled with cheers for the military, and more singing:

"Boro-bom-bom, boro-bom-bom,
Salí Galtieri, salí al balcón!"

General Galtieri then speaks to the people from the balcony of La Casa Rosada, the same balcony that Perón, Evita and

Isabelita used to address their supporters. General Galtieri proclaims that after 150 years of restrained emotion the noble Argentine people have finally recovered their beloved Malvinas. We all applaud him with much fanfare and fervour.

For the next 74 days, I'm glued to the radio and television, passionately celebrating every time a military communiqué reports that the glorious Argentine army has triumphed, or that the navy has sunk a 'pirate' ship, or that the air force has downed a British fighter jet… My blindness is such that I celebrate every British death and am deeply saddened by every Argentine casualty.

My attachment grows to the extent that I even turn up at the Ministry of the Interior's recruitment unit on Avenida Paseo Colón to volunteer. However, I'm made to wait for a long time in a seemingly endless queue and when my turn does finally come along the man charged with registering the volunteers says to me, "Sorry, kid, you're still too young. And besides, you're tiny. Go home, have your soup, grow up a little and then, if we're still at war, come back and I'll happily sign you up."

The rejection stings but by now I'm familiar with this sort of response so it certainly doesn't stop me from participating in this great and just national cause. I meet with groups of linguists to write letters in foreign languages that we send to different companies around the world urging their support. In these letters we express our legitimate right of sovereignty over the South Atlantic archipelago.

It's a tedious process. First we have to copy out by hand a model letter in English, Italian or French and place it in an envelope with the recipient's address written out neatly on the front. The next step is to head to the post office to have the letter weighed, making sure it doesn't exceed the 20gram limit. We then buy a stamp, run it across the tongue and stick it on the front of the envelope, to the top right of the address. Finally, once closed shut with the help of a little more saliva, we plant a sweet kiss on the important missive, in the form of a blessing, before popping it into one of the red postboxes Argentina received as a gift from the British government.

My war effort also leads me to use up my savings buying treats to fill little packages for the soldiers who've been sent to "our islands", in which I include personal letters of encouragement for the brave defence of our "beloved land".

At one point, two bright stars of Argentine television, Pinki and Cacho Fontana, organise a national collection. Thousands of people donate their savings, their jewellery and even their marriage rings to the great national cause: the recovery of not just the Malvinas, but also South Georgia and the South Sandwich Islands.

Our efforts continue in this way, even as we learn first of the terrible sinking of the General Belgrano cruiser, then of the failed intervention of Pope John Paul II, right up until the 14th June when Argentina surrenders and the British flag once again flutters over our Malvinas. My heart, along with that of millions of Argentines, is drowned with grief and I begin to foster a blind aversion to Britain. My obsession reaches the point that I won't eat any more sweets "Made in the UK".

A dilemma shortly arises, however, as I'm soon ready for my first shave and it's very hard to find any razor blades that haven't been made by the British. I don't know if that's the real reason I can't bring myself to shave or because, actually, I don't know how to do it, how to remove this fluff-like hair from my face, which is already quite noticeable above my upper lip. Some of my schoolmates laugh at my budding moustache, but I dare not ask them how to deal with it. Anyhow, besides the razor blade, I do know that I'm also in need of a razor, a brush, a mirror and shaving cream. For the time being, all I've got is half a mirror, cracked but still able to show me I'm maturing.
I wonder if the British encyclopaedia in the school library has an explanation on how to shave? How does one learn to shave? Who teaches you how to do this?

CHAPTER TWELVE
Rose
Liberal and stony

There's no longer any room for me in my mother's old shack; her new husband from Santiago del Estero and her two new children, plus the chickens, the new dog and my uncle Marcelo, together make it too crowded a space for us all to inhabit. But I feel like I don't really fit into this new family my mum is trying to build anyway, and there's no evidence it'll be a success either: the man drinks like a fish and certainly doesn't deserve her. For a while I drift between the homes of various school friends and from time to time stay with my grandparents, though of course I'm well aware of the inconvenience of my presence there and come to the conclusion that when you're not welcome somewhere the best thing you can do is not show up. Now that I have no place to call home any more, I start to wander more and more searching for a sense of belonging.

My great-uncle, Emilio Medolla Hübner, is brother to grandma Berta and is married to Esther, sister to Grandpa Pedro. This may seem a little odd to some, but not to me, because there's nothing wrong with a brother and sister marrying a sister and brother. It is a bit confusing, yes, but I assure you it's legal and not immoral in any way.

They live very comfortably in a beautiful house in San Isidro and have a large garden brimming with flowers whose persistently pleasant aromas offer a special welcome to all who approach the door of their house.

As their own son Jorge died very young and their daughter Beatriz is now happily married to a medical doctor and living in the centre of Buenos Aires, they kindly invite me to share their home with me, just around the corner from the racecourse in San Isidro: finally some love, in exchange for love alone.

Emilio truly is a monument to propriety, honesty, discipline, work and *buena onda* (good vibes!). I can't really say if he's behaving like a real father towards me because I don't have much of a father with which to compare him, but he does make me feel very comfortable in his home and is extremely generous to me. I sense he and Esther are learning to really love me as one of their own. I am a blood relation of both of them after all, in equal measure. They tell me that I remind them of their son and give me the bedroom that used to belong to him. Soon I too feel like another intimate member of their family.

One afternoon on my way to evening school in the centre, something catches my eye. As the yellow number 60 bus passes by Palacio de Congreso I notice that many wreaths of flowers have been laid on either side of the main entrance, just like the ones used to honour the dead, without their knowing. Or perhaps they do know.

The wreaths have been carefully placed at the edges of the steps to this beautiful palace, a building that closely resembles, in architecture alone, of course, the United States Capitol, the same one I've seen in American movies. It's a bizarre occurrence given that most people's eyes, mine included, are not accustomed to find any activity going on in National Congress whatsoever: the military has kept it shut for nearly eight years now. Curious, I approach a federal police officer to ask him what it's all about.

"They're for the funeral of Vicente Solano Lima", he replies.

"Who?"

"You know, the guy who was vice president of the Nation to Cámpora", he answers me dryly, then continues, "Don't you remember 'Cámpora to government, Perón to power'?" I give the impression I'm following his little history lesson and then, taking a deep breath to fill me with enough courage, I step inside the Blue Hall to pay my respects to this unknown, deceased, ex-vice president, who had been elected back in that distant time when people could still vote in Argentina. It's true I have some experience with the dead, as not many years earlier I held vigil next to the open coffin of Dr. Béccar Varela, but that paled in significance when compared to this funeral set-up, stocked full of wreaths whose scents now mingled with the days-old whiff of death.

Upon entering, my eyes are suddenly drawn to a tall slender old man, elegantly dressed, with a black ribbon tied around his left arm. He's standing next to the coffin, ceremoniously thoughtful. I recognise him immediately from a picture that appeared in the newspaper El Pregón: it's Jorge Antonio, the same man Uncle Emilio abhors for being, according to him, the figurehead of Perón. I'm well aware that Don Jorge is a very rich man and that he owns a magazine among many other possessions.

To continue my work at the new Festo Pneumatic headquarters and, at the same time, my studies is, as I mentioned before, becoming very tricky for me, especially seeing as the new company headquarters are even further away now. I really don't want to leave school because I promised myself to finish it, so I guess I have to think about changing jobs. All this springs to mind in a flash in this *mortuary* moment.

I guess I'd like to work on something related with journalism, perhaps at a magazine, actually. Having founded a monthly magazine at school called "De Paso por el Paso", which I continue to edit now, I realise that I really enjoy writing; particularly after a fantastic interview with the famous paediatrician Mario Socolinsky, an old alumnus of my school, who answered every one of my questions and even sang me his song *"na na na, na na na, na na na…"*.

I hurry out of the building, cross Avenida Callao and sit down on the steps of the monument in the Plaza de los Dos Congresos. I open up my black briefcase, take out a piece of paper and write out a note with my black pencil: "Señor Jorge Antonio, I'd really like the chance to speak with you. Tel. 743-9572, Esteban Cichello Hübner". I fold the little piece of paper several times and head back inside to the Blue Hall, feeling anxious but quite good.

Don Jorge Antonio is still standing there, perfectly upright, almost in a state of ataraxia, next to his dead friend, the former vice president of the Nation. I approach him slightly trembling now and, in front of hundreds of people, all in deadly silence, slowly position myself behind him.

His head is bowed and his hands held tightly behind his back, the left one clasped around his right wrist, leaving one palm open towards me. I'm sure he's adopting this pose in an attitude of reverence, and yet I sense it inviting me to proceed. As casually as possible, I creep up even closer, to the point where I can now touch him, the feeling of dread now very real and my legs shaking uncontrollably. I carefully extend my hand and place the small folded-up piece of paper into the centre of his palm. He feels it, automatically closing his fingers around it, then slides it meticulously into his pocket. Time now racing through my mind, I wonder how it's possible he hasn't yet looked round at me. Is it that he's accustomed to people passing him mysterious messages during a funeral?

This train of thoughts comes to an abrupt halt when Don Jorge finally turns his gaze towards me, rather deliberately, and asks with the purest of Iberian accents, "It contains your *señas*?"

"Yes", I reply in a hushed voice.

Fortunately, I know what *signs* means in this sense, a word hardly found at all in Argentina, but widely used in Spain to refer to personal information. Not wishing to linger any longer, I retreat a few steps without turning my back, as a sign of respect to both the deceased and the living. When I find myself outside again, I'm overcome with elation at having accomplished another important thing in my life.

I trot off to school straight away, managing not to mention anything to anyone for the whole time. When I arrive back at my uncles' house at around midnight, I immediately ask my provisional parents, "Has anyone called for me?"
"No one", they reply, in a natural tone.

Though I try not to show it, I'm a little disheartened. It's easy to imagine that Don Jorge Antonio isn't especially interested in calling up an impertinent brat like me, who asked him for an interview at his friend's funeral.
I repeat that same question several nights in a row, after arriving home from evening school, but I always get the same answer: "No Esteban, no one has called you."

I know Don Jorge Antonio must be a very busy man and that, like most rich and famous people, he doesn't have the time to do everything he'd like to do. He surely receives many of those little notes with all kinds of requests by people who recognise him in the street. He probably *can't* answer all of them, whether he's interested in doing so or not.

About three weeks later, having already completely forgotten about the affair in the Blue Hall and my contact request, I come in for a timely surprise.

Late one night, unlike previous occasions, stepping through the front door of my new home, I find Uncle Emilio wide awake waiting for me, along with Aunt Esther and her sister Rosa, all of them seated around the table in the dining room. There's a free chair waiting for me. Between the three of them, there's a total of 180 years of wise experience. I greet them as usual with a kiss to each; for some reason I don't think it will be necessary to ask if anyone called for me this time.

Uncle Emilio bids me sit down and I do so cautiously, while he tells me with the utmost gravity, his voice deep as ever, "Esteban, Señor Jorge Antonio called you."
"Ah yes! What did he want?" I ask innocently, as if it were totally normal to receive a call from Don Jorge Antonio. Then begins a round of inquisitorial questions.

"Esteban, who is this Jorge Antonio?"
"It's the same Jorge Antonio that you and everyone knows, Uncle. The very man himself", I respond defiantly.
Emilio hands me a piece of paper with a phone number on it. "Here's Don Jorge's office number". Silence.
Aunt Esther chimes in, "Why was he calling you?"
I don't answer.
Then Aunt Rosa tries, "How is it that this man has the phone number of this house?"
Still no answer, so Uncle Emilio continues, "Do you know what they say about Jorge Antonio? He's not a very nice fellow. He and Perón gave refuge to the Nazis who came

along the ratlines to Argentina after World War II. He himself even gave work to Adolf Eichmann, a genocidal anti-Semite and murderer, at his Mercedes Benz factory".

I silently think to myself about how Jorge Antonio and Juan Perón also opened the doors of Argentina to the Jews escaping the terrible Holocaust and all their other misery. It's far safer to shut up though and thereby avoid an argument.

My stream of thoughts pauses for a moment and now I feel the urge to tell them at least my story about the death and funeral of Vicente Solano Lima and the part where I put a little note into the right palm of Don Jorge Antonio, but again I refrain from speaking.

Uncle Emilio, and sisters Esther and Rosa, are members of the UCR (Unión Cívica Radical Party) and stout anti-peronists. They look me over suspiciously, their eyes revealing surprise at my cold silence. They must be worried I've gotten myself into something dodgy.

All this further adds to my usual reluctance to talk about what I'm up to. I prefer to remain silent, for *kabbalah*, at the best of times, and also because I'm afraid that if I do otherwise my schemes may fall flat. I'm not used to telling anyone about my plans until they actually materialise. I never let on, for example, when I have an exams or job interviews; I feel it's bad luck to talk about things before they happen so I only mention it afterwards if I pass or get the job! When I finally speak up, I manage to calm their late-night concerns assuring them that there's nothing weird going on, that I know perfectly well enough how to discern between good and evil, and that there is no reason to worry about a simple phone call from Don Jorge Antonio.

The following day I head out for work a little earlier than usual wearing my smartest clothes. I stop by a kiosk to buy myself a handful of ENCoTel *cospeles* (metal tokens) and queue up to the newly-installed orange pay phones at San Isidro train station. When it's my turn, I dial in Don Jorge's number and his secretary picks up at the other end inviting me for an interview with her boss on Avenida L. N. Alem, almost where it intersects with Avenida Córdoba, at 10 a.m. that very morning. I then speak briefly with Gabriela, the secretary at Festo, warning that I'll be a little late into work because of a job interview.

Leaving Retiro Central I set off walking towards L. N. Alem. I look up admiringly as I pass under the magnificent Kavanagh building, then making a right turn just before the Alas building, Argentina's tallest, to arrive perfectly on time to meet Don Jorge Antonio. My hair is well-groomed, my blue blazer patched and ageless on top of a white shirt, and a red tie my uncle Emilio gave me for use on special occasions like this.

I'm invited into the building with hardly a second to wait and as I enter Don Jorge's office I find him waiting for me standing in front of an enormous desk. His sheer presence exudes cleanliness. He shakes my hand firmly and then asks, "Tell me, young man, what brings you here?"

"Don Jorge, it is my dream to work for your magazine.

Then begins a bombardment of questions that are a joy to my ears, mostly due to the tune with which he strings them. His manner of speaking is leisurely and clear, with an unmistakable Castilian accent characteristic of a man of culture. He wants to know who I am, how I know him, where I live, where I was born, what I'm studying, what my parents do, where my grandparents are from, how old I am, what plans I have for when I finish studying, what work experience I have, the list goes on... And then suddenly I get one I wasn't prepared for in the slightest: do you know how to drive?

"No, no I don't. I never learnt, nor do I have any desire to, because", I pause, unsure how what I'm about to say will be received, "Don Jorge, it's my belief that I was in fact born to have a chauffeur, not be one myself".

He lets out a laugh, evidently caught off guard, and then replies, "Even if you *were* born to have a driver you should still learn how to drive. It's a very useful skill to have in life. I shall pay for your lessons".

Don Jorge Antonio, it turns out, is a good Muslim of Arab origin; as such, he explains to me that his payment for these lessons will be as a fulfilment of what he sees as his obligation to give *zakát*, which is not about giving charity, as is commonly believed, but doing justice, in Arabic and Hebrew alike.

"You, Esteban", he continues, "mustn't let a day go by without giving something to someone. However little you have, you must always help out your neighbour". His advice bears a strong resemblance to the teachings of my mother and Grandmother and keeps me nodding along all the while as I listen to him intently, watching his every move.

At length he picks up the black telephone on his desk and, without taking his eyes off of mine, dials in a number. He soon speaks into the phone saying, "Hello, Manolo, how's it going... I'm sending you a friend to work at the magazine. I want him on three days a week, no more, but pay him the full week; he also has to study... Yes, he's attending an evening school and saving up money to go to Israel, as well as helping out his mother and brothers... One more thing, please don't let the others know about this special arrangement, I don't want to cause any jealousy amongst the staff".

Don Jorge puts down the phone and scribbles down the address of his magazine on a little card. It's just around the corner from his office, on Avenida Córdoba, on the side of the even numbers. He then tells me to go and look for Sr. Manuel, gives me another firm handshake, thanks me for coming to see him and wishes me luck for my future.
I immediately set off to find Sr. Manuel and it's not long before he's welcoming me warmly into his office too, saying, "You are, from now on, an employee at a very fine place. Welcome, Sr. Esteban!"

I'm sad to give up my job at Festo Pneumatic, they were very good to me and even threw me a sweet little farewell party. Life at the new magazine where I work is very engaging though and I'm soon fully dedicated to learning how it's all put together. I mostly do small correction jobs, but there's a bit of office work and some marketing to be done too. Besides that, I'm paid really well and everyone treats me very kindly indeed.

Amongst a great many other things, I learn that the magazine was founded and edited through its first few years by a very impressive man, the journalist Don Jacobo Timerman, who the Military Junta forced to resign, persecuted, tortured and imprisoned. It's really quite an inspiring environment to be in, rubbing shoulders with people who think and debate all the time. It doesn't take me long to work out that all, or nearly all of them, are Peronists, praying for the next election to be won by the Italo Argentino Lúder-Deolindo Bittel ticket. It is, however, the radicals Raúl Alfonsín and Víctor Martínez who end up winning, at which point Don Jorge decides to close down the magazine. In spite of failure, there's a generous payout to all employees at the end, some of which I give to my mother, the rest I save up for my dream trip to Israel. Can I fulfill my dream of knowing Jerusalem and traveling the world? What does it mean not to fulfill a dream?

CHAPTER THIRTEEN
Reina
Magnificent and melancholic

Now I'm working as an office boy at an accounting firm called Jamondés, at 2600 Calle Teodoro García, near the corner with Amenábar, in the elegant central *barrio* of Belgrano.

It's a job my cousins Liliana and Mirian landed me. One of them is already an accountant there and the other is soon to finish her degree too. I take my orders from the secretary, a girl called Andrea Medicina, who's as organised as she is sweet. Her surname is like that of a hospital or a wealthy Italian family of patrons from the 16th century. Either way, I'm very fond of her.

My job is essentially to do whatever Andrea asks of me, such as going to the bank, the post office, the grocery store to buy coffee, tea or biscuits, sometimes even pastries, but nothing too fattening, as the girls are always on a diet. One eternal diet.

I'm also tasked with running errands to offices, client's houses, branches of the Directorate-General for Tax (known simply as DGI), and hundreds of banks and post offices all scattered across *Capital Federal.*
I'm transforming myself into an expert of my environment, every day furthering my mastery of the streets, bus routes and underground lines, as few office boys will have done before me. I'm constantly studying my *Filcar* map so that I can improve the way I travel. I soon know all of *Capital Federal* like the back of my hand, from Puente Saavedra to La Boca, Riachuelo to Liniers. I enjoy my work despite not

having the freedom to decide on much, as all the paperwork has to go under Andrea's eyes for approval.

I'm often happy to do the other girls a *"gauchada"*, or favour (lit. a show of *gaucho* solidarity), and occasionally for the boss' uncle too, as long as the stop is more or less on my way and I'm paid any extra expenses by them.

I learn a lot on my trips here and there, mainly to love and cherish the city of Buenos Aires itself: its French buildings, wide avenues, monuments, green squares (no railings!), elegant inhabitants, the men in their ties, the women their skirts and high heels. But a years-old obsession still lingers on in the back of my mind, unfulfilled: to reach the top of the Obelisk.

That horrible day, my first visit to *Capital Federal* is still fresh in my memory, when my ignorance led to a painful humiliation at the hands of my school's headmistress. Since then, I've always said to myself that one day I'll travel far and wide, discovering many places, not just Buenos Aires, but dozens of other cities and countries around this vast globe. I'm convinced that the Obelisk will be merely the first conquest of many and I dream that from its pinnacle I shall see the great bounds of my adoped city and beyond.

What I'm faced with is a structure nearly sixty-eight metres tall, grounded in the very heart of Buenos Aires, in the centre of Plaza de la República on Avenida 9 de Julio, an avenue so wide that it commands the respect of all pedestrians who are forced to pause mid-crossing under the imposing gaze of this majestic monument. One could say that the national significance of our Obelisk is akin to Paris' Eiffel Tower or London's Big Ben. Indeed, it is similar to that found in Washington and constitutes the third-highest of its kind in the world, divided into sixteen square concrete blocks with a small pyramid as its crown. It was built in 1936 to commemorate the founding of the city of Buenos Aires by the Spanish four hundred years earlier.

This well-erected monument explores the four cardinal points between the traditional Avenida Corrientes and Diagonal Norte, encircled on the ground by the shields of the twenty-three Argentine provinces.
Reaching its summit is a challenge worthy of my conquest. But...where to begin exactly? There's no public access.

Going about my various errands, I pass by it almost every day, ever more tempted to climb it somehow. I tell myself that, in conquering it, it will become a part of me; it will mean more to me than merely reaching the top of a monument: it will prove to myself that I can achieve the things that I set out to do.

Each time I pass by Plaza de la República I gaze at the Obelisk and wonder what it's like on the inside. Does it perhaps contain a super-fast elevator to whizz you to the top? Or is there a wide spiral staircase with hundreds of steps? What about its interior, is it clean and comfortable? Of course, the greatest mystery for me is how to actually go up it. There's nobody I know who's achieved it before and who I can turn to for advice. All there is a tiny door, about my height, on the side facing west, down Avenida Corrientes.

I've walked up to this door several times and tried to force it open, hoping to soothe my anxiety once and for all, but in vain: it's hard, strong, metal and elaborate-looking lock lends it an air of impregnability. I think I'll have to obtain a special permit, so I head to the Municipality to make enquiries.

The headquarters of the Municipal Government of the City of Buenos Aires is located on Avenida de Mayo, just across from the old Cabildo. I get as far as reception, where a man behind a desk greets me, "Good morning, how can I help?"

"Good morning, sir, I'd like to ask for a permit to go up to the Obelisk".

The receptionist looks at me sourly for a moment and then asks, "Look, kid, are you trying to have me on?"

"Absolutely not, sir!" I reply earnestly.

"Right, well, the Obelisk is off limits! Get it?" He says with a dismissive tone, followed by, "Now, bugger off, kid!"

He then gestures, raising his right hand up sharply, fingers extended and joined together, palm facing down, placing the tip of his index finger on the rim of his visor, just to the right of the eye. This is the first salute I've ever witnessed in person. He's looking past me, in fact, at the uniformed federal policeman who's acting doorman, standing stiff like a statuesque grenadier at the huge gate of the municipality.

I feel quite disturbed, unable to understand why this man is treating me so badly. To tell the truth, he does look a little simple, you can tell, but why all the rudeness? Even worse, however, is the copper who comes to kick me out. He suddenly bears down on me in a terrifying manner. It's surely just a ploy to get rid of me quicker. I dare not hang around to find out though.

I'm left thinking that perhaps the city mayor left explicit orders with this arrogant receptionist not to allow anyone to waltz in with any ideas like mine. Well, I can't be sure, but I do know that my request isn't so far-fetched. It's actually perfectly legitimate: I want to go up the Obelisk to see the full breadth of one of the most beautiful cities imaginable in this wonderful world. All I'm asking for is a permit, someone to simply open the door for me and let me go up and stay for a few minutes admiring the view.

I want to conquer the Obelisk. It's a desire that I've been carrying along inside me for a long time. It has evolved to such a point that I must now fulfill it so that I can start to believe in myself, that I really can do what I propose to do. I shall persevere. I certainly won't exactly give up at the first hurdle.

I'm going to ask Monica who works at the accounting firm with me; she knows quite a lot about the municipal offices.

"Tell me, Monica, a public monument, who exactly does it belong to?"

-What? Who does it belong to? Well, no one in particular, and then again, everyone, as in, all of us citizens. Why do you ask? Is it that you want to buy one?"

"No, I just want to know for the sake of general knowledge. But, anyway, who maintains the monuments?" I keep pressing her.

"How would I know, Esteban? I guess they're under the charge of the Municipal Department of Historical Monuments or the Museums Commission". She replies, obviously now quite fed up with my uncharacteristic questioning.

"Ah! Amazing! Thank you, Monica!" I reel off, before rushing down to the kitchen where I find my next target working away in the corner: Lucy Quispe (her surname is *aimara* and means precious stone), a lovely Ecuadorian brunette who often shares her lunch with me.

As soon as she sees me she says, "Come over here, Estebancito, try this. You're going to like it, I promise". Today she invites me over to taste ceviche for the very first time. She explains to me, in passing, that Ecuadorian ceviche far outranks the Peruvian one. Given that most of the time I go hungry during the day, I accept her invitation without a moment's delay, soon happily confessing to her how much I enjoy her creation: a fish dish with the bones already removed, a bit of onion and *jalapeño*, lots of lemon juice, tomatoes, salt, oil and a handful of *chifles* on the side. The sweet smell of lemon, mixed with other unknown and appetising spices makes my mouth water.

Lucy explains to me that the *chifles* are actually fried green banana slices. To get a rise out of her, I cheekily tell her that Peruvian ceviche surely tastes better. She looks at me for a moment and then laughs saying, "What do you know about Peruvian ceviche? I bet you've never come across a Peruvian in your life!"

"It's true, you're right, Lucy, I've never seen a Peruvian in my life; but, I do often listen to that Peruvian chatterbox, Hugo Guerrero Marthineitz on *Radio Rivadavia*, and he says that Peruvian ceviche is way better than any other in the world".

Lucy pulls a face but can't hold it for long and soon lets out a chuckle at my sharp response. She spends her days sat in front of a typewriter recording all the accounting entries and then listing them on copy paper for transcription into the large heavy ledgers. She works alone in the kitchen corner, accompanied only by the noisy tapping sound of her apparatus, and is usually quite curious to know what I'm getting up to. I tell her odd bits, taking care not to go into too much detail, afraid of jeopardising my great scheme regarding the Obelisk. She picks up on my reluctance to reveal my plans, worse than usual today, and puts on some music. Yet again, it's the latest cassette from Mercedes Sosa, and one song in particular that she leaves on repeat, *"Solo le pido a Dios... que el futuro no me sea indiferente..."* ("I only ask of God... that the future not be indifferent to me...").

In the office there's this new magic powder, called Nescafé, which you can dissolve in a cup of hot water, just a teaspoon of the stuff, and *bingo!* You have yourself a coffee. It's like a miracle coffee that Nescafé.

I make myself one with milk and then sit down to enjoy the caramelised aroma as it rises from my cup shaking off any residual drowsiness. I have two enormous volumes of the telephone directory for the City of Buenos Aires in front of me and I'm going to look up the address of that municipal department Monica was talking about.

I come to it soon enough and discover that it too is located on Avenida de Mayo. I'll go there at the first chance I get, I tell myself with the greatest resolve.
The days pass, the weeks too, while I hone my trade as urban scout, along with keeping up my studies at the evening school, from seven till ten thirty every night.

Leaving the office at five o'clock I usually head down the pedestrian street Florida. When I'm not in a hurry, I enjoy stopping a while to listen to the fiery political debates taking place on the corner of Lavalle Street. Almost every time I pass by I find dozens of people have flocked there to solve the country's woes with their words, sometimes with their fists too.

After having my fill of the commotion, I often walk a few blocks further down for a long chat with my octogenarian friend Vidalvina. She's completely blind, bless her, dressed in black, and I always find her sitting on the pavement outside Harrod's, begging for alms. I sit and chat with her, counting the coins she's collected during the day. Through her I learn that in London there's another Harrod's, even bigger and more beautiful, that's the older brother of this one. She also teaches me how to recognise the value of each coin according to the noise it makes when falling to the floor; her eyesight is next to useless but her hearing is as sharp as the sound of the coins themselves.

On other days I visit the library or, more often than not, peruse some bookshop where I never feel alone. In the library, I feel calm and free to pick up what I please; but in the bookshop, I can only read bit by bit, and in secret, because I'm always after new books that I can't afford. I wonder why books are so expensive in Argentina. I currently have books on the go at seven different spots and I know their locations exactly, returning every day to read another chapter.

Five of the bookstores are on Avenida Corrientes, the other two on Florida near the corner with Cangallo. Shifting between them in this way, reading for a short while at each place, I keep myself from being thrown out as a non-paying *leedor*, a freeloader, a cheat, and a non-buyer.

I use the word *leedor* and not *lector* because the great figure of the Spanish literature, the Argentine Don Jorge Luis Borges always likes being provocative with his use of language and often in his interviews speaks of *escribidores* and *leedores* (instead of the correct words *escritores* and *lectores*). I'm a big fan of this charmingly witty old man.

One day, I eventually let the cat out of the bag and tell some classmates at the evening school about my desire to ascend the Obelisk. They laugh in my face, mockingly advising me to get therapy to cure my stupid obsession with it. One boy who clearly doesn't like me much even says, "Esteban, you're a *nefelibato*, totally deluded. Do you really think they're going to let you go up there?"

I decide not to answer him. Two of my friends, however, Sergio and José, believe me and sign up for the big adventure.

It's been three weeks since the last wave of energy I invested in Mission Obelisk.

Today I'm finally going to the Municipal Department of Historical Monuments. Andrea sends me out to do some paperwork for the firm. I finish my task as quickly as possible and rush on to request the long-awaited permission to go up to the Obelisk.

I manage to speak to a man with a thickset moustache who introduces himself as the receptionist of the department. At first, he appears kind and happy to see me, but when I tell him of my intentions his eyebrows arch upwards abruptly and then his expression eases into an all-knowing smile as he comfortably explains that permits are only given out to students of architecture or photography, and not without delay either…

He goes on to say that, from what little he understands of my case, he doesn't think I fall into the category for permissions over which his department presides. The prattle continues as he offers up a great many other useless reasons, dressed in different guises, but it's all the same nonsense in the same silly falsetto voice. I remain patiently silent for as long as I can bear it, following the flippant flow until I grow tired of his blah blah blah and can muster enough courage to cut short the dreary soliloquy. At a moment's pause, I jump in, thanking him cordially for attending to me so graciously. I then add that despite being a student of letters, and therefore not automatically graced with the privilege of authorisation, I still want to go up the Obelisk and intend to do so with or without his help. At this, his eyes jump open in surprise, his bushy moustache twitching to the right. I swiftly turn around and leave.

The very next day I go to the Secretary of Culture for the Municipality of Buenos Aires in an attempt to hand in my application for permission there. I arrive at reception and promptly ask the employee, who's sitting behind a counter drinking *mate*, whether the Ministry of Culture is in charge of the Obelisk. Or perhaps I in fact asked whether the Obelisk is in charge of the Ministry of Culture. I begin to have doubts about how I actually expressed it when the man breaks into a sweet peal of laughter. After pulling himself together again he says, "I'm not sure. We'll have to find out".

He fetches a black folder containing a few sheets with a long list of names; then, passing his finger from top to bottom, page after page, he reads some of the names out loud, mumbling others; a few are familiar to me: "Teatro Colón, Teatro Presidente Alvear, Teatro San Martín,

Zoological Garden, School of Dramatic Art, The Planetarium, National Historical Museum, ta, ta, ta… No, *che* (you) no, the Obelisk doesn't belong to us, I'm afraid, nor we to it. Why? You want to buy it?"

"I'd like to rent it actually", I answer, forcing my best smile.

Before turning to leave, I give him a military salute, something I've curiously grown inclined to do for certain people whose treatment I've appreciated, raising my right hand up to my temple, in a show of honour and love for patria. Of course, I've only adopted the salute, not the attitudes the men who perform it. I think they've scared me enough already.

I can't seem to forget that day I was given a good kicking at the Community Centre, round the corner from my old home. Nor can I erase from my memory the other more recent day I spent marching arm in arm with the Mothers of the Plaza de Mayo, when the military beat us all mercilessly —those mothers who were only calling for the safe return of their *disappeared* children, who wore white handkerchiefs on their heads that had been so painfully embroidered with the names of their children and the date of their disappearance.

A few women started out by gathering to protest in the main square in silence. However, the police told them they weren't allowed to stay there; that, at the very least, they had to move about. That's why they started walking around the Pirámide de Mayo, right in front of the Casa Rosada, the seat of the National Executive Branch. The mothers continuously joined together in these slow ponderous laps around the Plaza de Mayo every Thursday, repeating their just and moving claim, such that the few voices gradually grew into a broad movement of protest.

One such Thursday, as I'm marching side by side with these brave women in peaceful defiance, a group of mounted police charges into us, swinging indiscriminately at anyone in their path. A canister of teargas narrowly misses my shoulder. The severe stinging leaves me practically blind. I stumble and fall to the ground passing out. An hour or so later, I wake up inside a building on Diagonal Norte, between Esmeralda and Cangallo, right in front of the monument to Don Lisandro de la Torre. I'm lying on one of the steps of a marble staircase with my head resting on the lap of a mother who's mopping my face with her wet white handkerchief, the stitches of her son's name passing over my eyes, and fanning me from time to time thus relieving the burning sensation on my face. I blame the military first and foremost for the blaze in my eyes and secondly for the mess in which our country finds itself.

***

Today I bought my first camera. I know it's a good one because it was made in Japan. I originally wanted a Polaroid, one for taking snapshots, but seeing as I couldn't afford it I settled for a simpler Kodak camera. It uses a small film that takes colour photos and as it's imported each one costs me a small fortune. That's not to mention the camera itself, simple though it is; half my monthly salary as an office boy is spent on it. But I want to be better equipped for my mission to the top of the Obelisk. I'm more than happy to deprive myself of certain things in the meantime: gastronomic delights, trips to the cinema, bus rides whose distance I can easily cover on foot. I dream of taking a beautiful shot from each of the four cardinal points, through the four little windows of the pyramid at the head of the Obelisk.

I know my work at the accounting firm is only temporary, but it's perfect since it allows me time to study and to bring me closer to this wonderful city at the same time.

Buenos Aires is a city that's very congested with its nearly three million inhabitants, and then there are another two million who arrive every day for work. It's crammed full of cars that choke it in toxic gases and hysteria, in equal parts. People aren't particularly friendly. What's more, there are homeless people living in the every corner of the place, and many children begging too. It's especially upsetting to see so many old people sleeping out exposed to the harshness of the elements. And then of course there are other lamentable realities, like people puffing away on buses and trains. Thank heavens smoking is at least forbidden on the subterranean!

The underground network here isn't extensive, made up of

only five lines, and therefore it's nearly always crowded, resulting in an unpleasant experience at the best of times. Yet, during the summer months, the sweat, humidity and other foul smells all combine to make it near unbearable, especially during rush hour.

To wait in the queues to the ticket offices where you have to purchase the aluminium tokens needed for your trip often feels like facing eternity itself. It's hard to work out why people don't just buy the little coins in bulk instead of one at a time. I guess it's because they just don't have enough money.

Fortunately for me, since the office pays for my travel expenses, I'm able to buy the tokens in a blister pack of ten, meaning that more often than not I can avoid the long queues every time I'm sent out on a mission.

The city's pavements are in places non-existent, but worse still are the loose slabs, which, even in the slightest drizzle, quickly become treacherous to all outfits, creating a number of threats and much hesitation. Out in the middle of the streets, the roads are strewn with potholes and buses venting thick wafts of black smoke from their exhaust pipes, with passengers hanging out of their open doors.

In the endless queues at bus stops, especially those in the down-town area, it's curious to find men letting all the women onto the buses first, momentarily suppressing their machismo. I'm actually quite sick of waiting for buses in the proximity of some girl's high school as I always seem to get stuck behind a *machista* wanting to play the gentleman and, along with all the other men in line behind him, am invariably compelled to travel standing up. This discriminatory kind of gallantry seems totally wrong to me. Women of course deserve to be treated with respect, but in a deeper and more genuine sense, not a superficial one, like allowing them to board the bus first.

There are times I think that some men were only put on this earth because there has to be a bit of everything; but not all of them are worth something, and some of them really are worthless. The latter seem to exist only so that they can lord it over women, dominate them in every way possible, making them feel like hostages in their own homes, and, when they get drunk, inflicting on them their deepest instincts in the form of violence and also death. I've seen those kinds of men up close, in my own home.

There are a great many other things I can't get my head around in Buenos Aires, like, for example, why cops and priests don't pay the travel fare. Don't they too have a salary and work just as much as teachers, doctors and office boys? It doesn't seem very fair. I can understand soldiers on military service not paying because they have low wages, but I feel that coppers and priests have no excuses.

Buenos Aires is, despite its name, a city lacking in *good air*. It does, however, retain a special charm. Indeed, it's impossible not to be captivated by its glamour, its style, and its people. Though generally speaking I find the actual *porteños,* those native to the city, a little pretentious and unfriendly, the blend with people from the interior, like me, and foreigners who've also come to make the city their home allows for a more harmonious cohabitation.

The *porteños* have an undoubtedly arrogant tone that comes off somewhat stuck up. I myself unfortunately no longer speak with the *Cordobés* accent I grew up speaking, though the sweet tune of that provincial accent still occasionally rolls off my tongue. I'm now learning to speak more and more like the locals, *al verre,* swapping around the syllables of certain words to make new slang, like *yeca* (from *calle,* street), *tordo* (from *doctor*), *sopes* (from *pesos*), *jermu* (from *mujer,* woman), *tagui* (from *guita,* money). I also use phrases to do with money like, 'I don't have a *mango*' (cent), or, 'it cost me five *palos*' (sticks, i.e. five million pesos) and 'two *lucas*' (two thousand pesos). There's no doubt in my mind Buenos Aires has *swing*.

Today I have another personal errand to run after work and something tells me it could be a special day. While following my usual route to *laburo* (work), two of the three buses I take give me tickets with palindrome numbers; one of them is 779977, which strikes me a particularly lucky number that I get in the bus number 541 when traveling to Lomas de Zamora.

My mind drifts as I admire the way the bus drivers cut out each ticket specific to the passenger's destination—there are often about twenty different fares for each bus—but they also have to give out change, look in the mirror, be attentive and mindful to what's going on around them, drive (obviously), and many of them are doing all of that while smoking a cigarette at the same time! They're excellent at multitasking, that's for sure, truly admirable.

A little later in the day, I find myself on another bus, this time to the Directorate for Green Spaces, a branch of the Municipal Department for Environment, which is located near the Planetarium. Here I shall continue on my quest to conquer the Obelisk. But first I'm going to eat a pizza at Pizzería Güerrin, 1300 Avenida Corrientes. Will taking out two palindrome tickets be a harbinger that I am going to be doing well today? How attentive are we to see the happy omens?

CHAPTER FOURTEEN
Malvina
Unattainable and voluptuous

Today I have lots of errands to run in the big 'urb' (I like the word *urbe* because it sounds like *ubre*, which means 'udder'), however I decide to make a short detour to the municipal office in charge of Park Maintenance in *La Reina del Plata* ("The Queen of Río de la Plata"), as Buenos Aires is sometimes called on the radio. When I arrive at the building a striking secretary attends me who, despite her age—she must be around sixty years old—is the embodiment of voluptuousness. I immediately fall under the spell of her Isabel Sarli-esque breasts.

Sarli was the national star of a quasi-pornographic genre of films. One line of hers often comes to my mind: in the film *Fever* she says to her beloved co-star Armando Bo, "Pleasure me like the stallion pleasures his mare...": words that kept me awake many long nights trying to understand them.

The woman now before me, her fleshy lips painted a deep purple-red, across which passes a delightful accent from the provinces, somewhere between Tucumán and Santiago del Estero I'd say, speaks with carefree sympathy, drawing me irresistibly into her realm, almost conquering the aspiring conqueror...

At length, I manage to snap out of her spell and explain why I've come to her office. She listens nonchalantly, nodding along to every word I utter, her mouth slightly ajar, but I'm not actually sure she's really following; either that, or perhaps my request for permission to climb the Obelisk is a totally common occurrence there. I don't know.

Then I drift off again as I'm speaking and it's as if she's genuinely acquiescing to my every desire, right here and now, with all the naturalness in the world. I find myself quickly wanting her to be the final arbiter of my fate. When I finish pouring my heart out, she softly asks me to wait a few minutes and slips away leaving a delicious scent hanging in the air she's just vacated.

She's left the office completely now, and yet that sweet smell gives me the sense that her presence lingers on around me. I can tell her perfume is *Charlie*, because it's distinctively fruity and fresh, and also because I've tried out a free sample of it in *Ivonne* on Florida Street, near Avenida Corrientes. As I frequently pass by there, I sometimes stop for a few minutes to play a game with myself: the aim is to take a whiff of the samples and try to guess the different brands of each one, while keeping my eyes closed. I've become so good at it I rarely make a mistake these days! And it's true, of course, that office boys have plenty of free time on the job…

A few minutes pass and the scented secretary returns to beckon me through to the manager's office. I make a ceremonious entry and place myself right in front of his desk. He squeezes my hand firmly and invites me to sit down. My first impression is that he's a really cool guy, his wise old face full of geniality. He introduces himself as Aldo González and tells me his secretary has already made him aware of my desire to go up the Obelisk. He then says, "Why do you want to go up there?"

"It's been my dream for ten long years, *señor*", I tell him unwaveringly, staring him straight in the eye. "It's something I simply must do so that I can believe that what I set out to do is achievable".

I'd rather not tell him the story of my first trip to Buenos Aires and the humiliation that's stayed with me all this time. I'm afraid he wouldn't understand and it might even mess up my chances unnecessarily; indeed, this kind old man might well think that, instead of going up the Obelisk, I should really go and see a psychologist like many other thousands of Argentines do daily.

"Listen, kid, the Obelisk is mine... I mean it belongs to my jurisdiction... I am in charge of it, so to speak, and I would have no problem whatsoever in letting you make your desired ascent to the top of it". At this point, he pauses for effect, and then continues, "But there's a catch... Though it may sound like I'm lying to you, I don't actually have the keys and, honestly, I don't know *who* has them. You'll have to forgive me but without keys you ain't getting in, unless you can fly in through one of the windows at the top". He flaps his arms like a bird.

His candour is disarming and the whole flying motion has me chuckling. He's acting pretty silly, but there's something about him that inspires confidence: his honest face appears to me like that of a benevolent grandpa.

I say goodbye to Sr. González thanking him for his time and leave the building, regrettably without finding out *her* name, the bewitching secretary.

I've never felt so good though. How wonderful it feels to be alive! This really is my lucky day, heralded by that pair of palindrome tickets which greeted its beginning. The long winding path up that tall tower of white stone is finally taking on some more colour and another dimension to me.

I'm practically convinced that Sr. González is a man of his word, but I must now overcome one final obstacle to unlock my dream. Yes, I'm truly happy, I tell myself, but how the hell am I going to find that key? It's an inner call that has no answer as yet, such is the depth of the mystery.

***

Today I'm up nice and early, having spent the night over at my friend Nicanor's apartment on Suipacha 700. I've been tasked with paying in a couple of checks for license plates and car tax in Banco Ciudad on Carlos Pellegrini Street. I head out, first crossing the street to the kiosk to pick up a copy of *Crónica*, one of my favourite papers.

I'm still riding the same wave of optimism on this cold sunny morning, dressed in my best clothes: grey trousers, white shirt, blue blazer and burgundy tie. Incidentally there's not a patch on me and I feel all the more complete for it!

In this branch, as is quite common outside banks in Buenos Aires, the queues are enormous, sometimes covering more than two blocks.

At ten to seven, I walk briskly down Suipacha Street until reaching Avenida Corrientes, where I turn right towards 9 de Julio and instinctively greet my friend, the unchanging Obelisk, with a customary salute as he comes into view. I get the impression he's winking back at me from one of his four eyes at the top. I smile back, and then look up at the electronic clock outside Banco Ciudad showing 7 o'clock on the dot.

A van parked up on Plaza de la República catches my eye; it certainly isn't a familiar sight, with its back doors flung open. A sturdy-looking man, short in stature like me, sweeps nearby on the square. I watch him for a while from the publishing house *Kapelusz*, on the North East corner of Avda. Corrientes and Carlos Pellegrini. Eventually I assure myself there's nothing to lose and cross the street like a train at full throttle, approaching this shy-looking man with only one thing on my mind. After greeting him, I look him directly in the eyes and ask, "Tell me, *señor*, who has the keys to the Obelisk?"

He looks at me with a clean, full and healthy face, replying respectfully, but with a lispy voice lacking in confidence, "Hello there, young sir… Ehhh, look, I'm not too sure, maybe… Look for engineer Becerra, yes, talk to him, hey, maybe he knows. I don't have them… I don't know anything, please forgive me".

He has a thick Bolivian accent, one of my favourites. If I'm not mistaken, his speech is suffused with tones typical of the Aymara language. In any case, I'm quite sure Spanish isn't his first language and, if I had to say, I'd guess he's from Cochabamba, because he speaks just like my friend Willy Mamani's mum who's from there.

I promptly open up my black briefcase where I keep all my papers, the accounts payable to Banco Ciudad, and my copy of *Crónica*. I take out my Citanova diary and copy the inscription on the side of the van:
S.A.D.E. Barrido y Limpieza (Sweeping and Cleaning)
"Mantenga Limpia su Ciudad" (Keep Your City Clean)
Phone 857-0908

No sooner have I finished than I feel another pang of happiness. I just sense it's another big step towards achieving my dream.
I then look up at the Obelisk, standing there coldly erect, somewhat indifferent to my plans. I'm at his feet, unrelenting, and I say to him, "Soon you shall be mine, dear Obelisk. We shall be together and embrace each other at long last".

While waiting more than two hours in the sluggish queue to the bank, I start trying to plot my next move.
I pay the fines and then take line D on the underground all the way to its terminal station, Plaza Italia.

On the way, I reflect on why it was that the kind municipal worker answered my question so willingly; in my experience, people aren't usually so forthcoming. I wonder whether perhaps it was because he noticed my blue blazer, burgundy tie and briefcase, and thought I resembled some figure of authority. Or perhaps, standing in the sheltering shadow of the lofty Obelisk inspired me, imbued me with a timely vein of authority that helped me prize out the valuable piece of information I craved and dared hope would lead me to its peak. Was it a matter of fate in action, or me simply forging my own destiny? Either way, I count it as another miracle.

I arrive at my office brimming with hope, and earlier than usual too. The wonderful start to my day is soon supplemented by the news that Jamondés, owner of the firm, is not coming to work today. I hear some of the girls say he's having a row with his wife, over another piece of skirt. Apparently this time he's going out with someone they know. They say he went to the drive-in cinema with his own niece last night and that his wife was none too pleased about it. At least he kept it in the family, I think to myself… I saw this eye-catching niece a number of times; she looks like she could be one of the *Trillizas de Oro* ("Golden Triplets"), those beautiful blonde girls who appear on television. I can easily picture Jamondés at the drive-in with his arm around any of them.

The owner's uncle is a man named Don León, a punctilious

suck-up and the second in command at the firm. As a bold informer to his nephew, it's also a relief for me to hear that he too won't be coming in today due to falling foul to a bad cold. That's nothing out of the ordinary though. It's quite normal for him to spend the entire day sneezing, wheezing and noisily blowing his nose into an ever-present handkerchief at least three times an hour. He deposits this slimy green substance onto the handkerchief, which he then neatly folds and places into the outer pocket of his brown jacket, his apparently only jacket.

He's cool with me, to be honest, but a bit of a grass all the same. We have to be extra careful with what we say and do around him.

Those two being absent, I can confidently expect a leisurely day ahead, for me especially, seeing as Andrea says there are hardly any errands to run today, and the few there are aren't urgent.

The thought of this unanticipated liberty is thrilling at first, but I soon start to tire of hanging around the office. I don't know what to do with myself, free from all the usual restraints, fearless of being caught in the act, either fooling about or being unashamedly idle.

Finding myself at my wits' end and feeling compelled by the circumstances, I decide to enact another step in my plan, *Obelisk (once and for all)*', albeit with a few alterations. Unable to actually leave the office and visit S.A.D.E. myself to inquire about this engineer Becerra in person, it occurs to me that I can do so just as easily from here, on the phone.

I realise I'm going to need my cousin Liliana Esther's help; she's an obvious choice as we've always seen eye to eye. She's the only member of my father's side of the family who'd been to the shack where I used to live. We never talk about it, but I get the sense she's impressed by the way her younger cousin has grown up.

I've noticed that ever since that visit she's always treated me differently, trying to spoil me, and I love her for it. With this in mind, I very discreetly go and ask her to follow me into our boss' office for a quick chat, in absolute privacy. She agrees and, once inside, I present to her my master plan.

"Liliana, I need you to call this number for me". I hand her a note with the number 857-0908 on it. I continue, "Please call up and just ask to speak with *Ingeniero* Becerra. Once you have him on the line, tell him, 'Just a moment, please, Sr. Esteban Cichello Hübner would like to speak to you about a matter for the Municipality of the City of Buenos Aires".

"What little scheme is this, Esteban? What are you getting into exactly?" She asks me, though she cares not for my answer, as she instantly picks up the phone, to my surprise, and follows out my plan to the letter. On top of that, she turns out to be quite perfect for the role, even lending a certain tone of suspense to her voice.

A secretary answers the call, at which point Liliana

introduces herself as *my* secretary and asks for the engineer, passing me the receiver when he comes on the line.

I take it assuredly, first covering the microphone with my hand, pausing for a few long seconds to think about what I'm going to say. That's when I realise another miracle is about to happen…

"*Holaaaa*", I say dryly, my voice almost gruff. Then, cutting the usual formalities, I venture a little further, "*Ingeniero* Becerra?"

"Yes", comes a slightly broken voice from the other end, one which doesn't pause for long, "I know why you've called, Dr. Sichel (he calls me doctor?!). You'd like the keys to the Obelisk, correct?" When I hear this, I almost drop the receiver to the floor. The shock has my heart beating loudly in my ears; I can't find any words to utter back so I opt instead for a series of *um-hum* sounds to convey my agreement. My mouth is almost closed shut and I suck the air in through my nose. Meanwhile Becerra continues verbosely, "Forgive me, Dr. Sichel, you must forgive me", his voice now marked by a tone of guilt and constraint, "It's just that when Pope John Paul II came to Argentina during the Falklands-Malvinas War, you remember, don't you, Doctor, he was going to give a great mass from the Obelisk and, well, I was in charge of building the huge platform for the occasion and that's why I requested the keys to the Obelisk from you. However, at the last moment, the curia decided to hold the mass at the *Monumento de los Españoles* so I kept hold of the keys. Throughout this time I had every intention of returning them to you, of course, but between one thing and another I never got round to it. I do apologise, Dr. Sichel, I'll have them sent to you right away with a runner boy".

"No, no", I reply confidently. "Please don't bother yourself, Ing. Becerra, I'm sending my own office boy over to you right now to pick them up".

"Well, alright then. Tell him to come to Pacheco de Melo 2703".

"Okay, fine, he'll be with you shortly. Until next time, *ingeniero*", I end the conversation.

"Goodbye, Dr. Sichel. And, once again, forgive me for the inconvenience". He ends the call.

I hang up the receiver and immediately let out a cry of joy that catches my dear cousin, the fine amateur actress, Liliana, totally off guard. The poor girl has no idea what's going on and is intrigued to find out the content of our conversation. I invoke the *kabbalah* once again, explaining that I don't want to jinx my luck, but that in a few days she'll certainly know everything there is to know about that phone call. Liliana understands and leaves it at that. How wonderfully discreet she is!

I then go over to ask Andrea Medicina for permission to go out on a quick personal errand. I'm desperate to get to Ing. Becerra's office as fast as is humanly possible.

Permission granted. I rush out and board straight onto a green 59 bus, taking it to Avenida Las Heras from where I walk the rest of the way to Pacheco de Melo. I count along, building by building, until I reach 2703. It's an office. I present myself at reception as an office boy for the Municipality of Buenos Aires who's come to pick up the keys to the Obelisk. The receptionist makes a quick internal call and then asks me to wait a moment. After a few minutes, a woman appears introducing herself as Ing. Becerra's secretary. In her hands is a brown coloured paper envelope addressed to Dr. Sichel, Municipality of Bs.As. She hands it to me saying, "Please tell Dr. Sichel that we really are extremely apologetic for any trouble caused".

"I will", I reply and turn to leave the building at a normal pace, maybe even a little slower than usual, so as not to arouse any suspicion.

Once out in the street, now far from the S.A.D.E. office, I open up the envelope and there she is: this big, heavy, solid and silvery key. She certainly has an impressive character, quite slender, measuring about twelve centimetres long, with a broad head, elegant grooves along her flat sides, and a series of notches underneath varying in depth and length. The more I look at her and hold her in my hands the more majestic and heraldic she appears to me. Weighing a little over a hundred grams, she seems perfectly suited to my grip; and at the same time, I sense her clinging onto me as much as I am her, as if thanking me for having rescued her from those senseless people who'd held her captive, languishing and forgotten. I then notice she did not come to me alone but accompanied by a few words written in blue ink:

"Doctor Sichel, please forgive me. I am always at your service, Becerra".

I give out a huge cry of '*Viva Bolivia and Cochabamba!*' and, just in case I'm messing up the accent of my dear *Saint Peter* from the square, send out a few more hurrahs for La Paz, Sucre, Potosí, Santa Cruz de la Sierra and a final one for Simon Bolivar himself; indeed his name was given to the nation of that friendly sweeper in the Plaza de la República to whom I owe such gratitude.

I then return the key to the envelope and place it deep into the inner pocket of my blazer, safe at last and close to my heart. I now have to rush back to my workplace, overwhelmed by some ineffable new feeling within me. I decide it's best to cut any further delay and take a taxi, thereby allaying any lingering suspicions about my absence.

In the end, no one even sees me enter; the girls are still whispering and chittering over one another about Sr. Jamondés and his lovers, the same as when I left. No one suspects a thing, I'm completely ignored: just how I want it!

I remain anxious for the rest of the day, until it's time to go home. I'm tempted to go straight away and conquer the Obelisk but in the end refrain from giving more fuel to this crazy idea, deciding instead to skip my evening classes and head straight home as soon as possible.

I'm not living with my great-uncle and aunt anymore because my aunt Esther got breast cancer, at which point they needed my room for the carers who were looking after her following the operation. I said goodbye to them full of appreciation; Uncle Emilio was the closest thing to a father for me. But it's over. I'm now back at my mum's house, where we're practically living on top of each other.

I take the yellow 60 bus back up the Pan-American Highway again. Several times during the trip I find myself feeling inside the inner pocket of my blazer with the tip of my fingers, just to make sure the key is still there, nestled against my heart. My brain is ticking over and over as I try to come to terms with the fact that I, a starry-eyed squirt, am carrying home this glorious key to perhaps the most famous and emblematic monument of the Argentine Republic.

I finally arrive at the shack, greeting my dog Toti and my mum with a kiss. I am asked why I'm not in school (just to be clear, it is my mum asking me, not Toti, because he often speaks to me too, but with his gaze). I lie saying, "There were no classes today. They were cancelled due to a bomb threat".

There's nowhere to hide, however, as we all share a single room, which acts as dormitory, kitchen and living room combined. Thus I'm unable to escape the small, black, inquisitive eyes of my little brother Marcos David, the large, deep-set eyes of my little sister Claudia Noemí, the indifferent eyes of my uncle Marcelo, the ever-sorrowful eyes of my beloved mother, and the faithful, ever-cheery eyes of my dog Toti.

Despite all these sets of eyes staring at me, I manage to sneak the envelope with the key belonging to my friend, the Obelisk, under my pillow. Everyone suspects I'm up to something but they can't figure it out and don't dare to ask me either. It suits me perfectly; I don't want to face any questions.

I want night to fall as soon as possible so that I can lie down and think peacefully in the darkness, try to figure out some details of my next steps. I'm usually a night owl, but I need an early night this time. Realising that neither thinking nor sleeping is going to be easy in an icy cold bed, I first go and heat up a sand brick in the embers. When it's hot enough, I then wrap it in newspaper and return to my bed, tucking it in with me between my feet.

I take further comfort when noticing Toti looking up at me tenderly, full of loyalty, curled up on the floor at my side. My thoughts can finally run free. I figure out that, although I'm definitely up for going it alone and opening the door to the Obelisk by myself if I have to, it could be a little risky. I fear there's a good chance the police might see me, stop me and drag me off to jail, effectively ending my hard-fought conquest.

I say a quick prayer thanking God for today's miracle, feel for the key one last time, caressing it, filling up with pride and finally fall sound asleep dreaming happily of my prize, so close now I can almost touch it.

Out of caution, I let another two days pass by without saying a word to anyone. At all times, the key is there hanging around my neck on a black shoelace, as if it were some cherished reward I had attained through merit.

Though I can always feel it rubbing lightly against my chest, it's not enough; I can't help myself touching at it through my clothes, sensing each time I do that it's becoming more and more mine.

Today is Thursday, my lucky day, and I'm keen to go and see Sr. Aldo González again, the head of Park Maintenance in the Municipality of the City of Buenos Aires. He's the man who told me a few days ago, with a great sense of compassion, how he understood my wish to go up to the Obelisk, and that he himself would authorise me to do so in a heartbeat, if I could just find the whereabouts of the only key to that great armoured door.

At around three o'clock in the afternoon, I turn up at Sr. González' office, near the Planetarium. There's no hiding the huge smile across my fresh-looking face as I stand before the desk of the same explosive good looks of the older lady who is his secretary. My smile is not, however, reciprocated this time, and so taking a deep breath to draw out any reserves of courage I announce to her, "Good afternoon, my name is Esteban, the kid who came to enquire about the Obelisk". She nods, as if confirming she remembers me, and then her fleshy lips quiver for a moment—they're painted a deep red this time, contrasting with her bright pearl-like teeth—before finally shaping into a seductive smile. I start up again, "Forgive me, but I can't remember your name".

"Malvina", she replies, as I stare into her big beautiful black eyes. A short silence ensues. I'm baffled, to tell the truth. For some unknown reason, I never expected that to be her name. Both of us, it would appear, then realise that her name didn't come up in conversation at our previous meeting.

A whole series of images flash through my mind at this point: Las Malvinas (The Falkland Islands), Malvina Pastorino, actress wife of another famous actor Luis Sandrini, and Malvina the greengrocer neighbour of my paternal grandparents at Calle Jacinto Diaz in San Isidro. I was expecting a beautiful woman like her to be called Graciela, as in Borges; or Moria, as in Casán, or Susana, as in Giménez; or Rafaela, as the Carrá; or Sandra, as in the character played by Isabel Sarly in the film *Fever*, but certainly not Malvina…

"Well, in that case, Sra… Malvina, I would very much like to see Sr. Gonzalez if possible. I have something for him", I tell her, still a little disconcerted.

I show her the brown paper envelope that I obtained from engineer Becerra, through his secretary, containing the key to the Obelisk, along with his personal apology note.

Malvina asks me to wait a few minutes, indicating with an open hand an armchair opposite her desk. Her bright red nails catch my eye. She then stands up, revealing as she does so a pair of translucent white trousers, through which I notice her long slender legs, mounted at the bottom on red stiletto shoes. Her hips shift smoothly from side to side as she walks. Not knowing why, I turn red too, feeling an unexpected heat taking hold of me bit by bit.

Malvina isn't gone long before returning to open the door to an adjoining office. She looks at me again, smiling, and says with her metallic sensual voice, "Esteban, this way, please".

"Thank you very much, Sra. Malvina", I say, waiting once again to see if she corrects me and tells me to call her '*Señorita* Malvina', but she doesn't. Perhaps she's married, a thought that further troubles my already muddled head.

I enter the office to find the kind honest face of Sr. Gonzalez, who's shorter than I remembered and almost completely bald too. Without taking his eyes off me for a second, he shakes my hand asking, "Young Esteban, what brings you here this time?"

I say nothing. Instead, in total silence and suspense, I slide the brown paper envelope across his desk.

Sr. González looks me in the eye, then down at the envelope; he picks it up, feels it, opens it, draws out the key and reads the card. After a while, he looks up again and asks me, "What's all this about? Tell me, please… I can hardly believe it's what I think it is!"

"Well, *señor*, you told me you'd let me go up the Obelisk if only you had the key… And, well, here it is, the key to the

Obelisk itself".

He stares at me full of surprise, with a hint of disbelief too, and before he can bombard me with questions I tell him all about how this most precious of artifacts came to be in my possession. I tell him of that cold sunny morning on which I met that wonderful Bolivian sweeper in the Plaza de la República and of my cheeky phone call to the engineer Becerra. I give him the full account, in all its chronological detail.

González listens along carefully, a permanent smile printed on his face. At times he has to make a real effort not to burst out laughing, but when I finish narrating my story, he lets loose a loud and raucous guffaw that immediately summons the Sra. /Srta. Malvina into the office. She comes right over to us, curious to find out what's going on; at which point González gets out of his chair and gives me a huge and joyful hug. He then turns to Malvina and relates the whole story I've just told him. He concludes by saying, "*Malvi*, take all of Esteban's details and then give him all of ours, including our home telephone numbers, everything. We're going to send him to the tip of the Obelisk! He's more than deserved it! And he's saved us a lot of time and money too… There'll be no need to break down the door any more, that's for sure. I can't believe it, it's the very same one: serrated, impossible to copy… You know the lock on that door is impossible to pick too… Esteban is a true hero of the city!"

"Ah! Esteban", he continues after a short pause, "Please choose the day you like, preferably a Sunday—because on Sundays there's less activity in the Plaza—organise a group of friends who you want to take with you, and think of a useful pick-up point. I'm going to send you a special van from the Municipality. I'll also be sending a patrol car and an ambulance, just in case, to avoid any issues. Just please don't tell anyone how you got the keys to the Obelisk…"

"Don't worry, *señor*, my lips are sealed", I reply, expressing my deep appreciation to him with a firm handshake, and then off I go.

Malvina walks me to the main door and gives me a farewell kiss on the cheek, leaving a warm mark there with her crimson lipstick. Her perfume stays stuck to my clothes for several sweet hours after. I'm over the moon, but not because I've moved ever closer to getting what I want; that's not the happiness I really seek; what makes me happiest of all is to cherish what I already have, enjoy it and share it with others. Will I be able to share with others my dream of reaching the top of the Obelisk? What does it means to share a dream?

CHAPTER FIFTEEN
Luz
Distant and accessible

I return to the office overflowing with joy. I'm already picturing myself at the top of the Obelisk looking out through its windows at the four cardinal points of my adoptive city.

The first thing I do is tell my cousin Liliana. She listens in silence, a pretty smile etched across her face, and readily accepts my offer of adventure, wishing to invite her boyfriend Rodrigo too. It so happens my other cousin Miriam is tuning in on this conversation, but when I extend to her the invitation, she isn't so enthused by the idea.

I get the impression that, as she's a bit older than us, she thinks she's above it all, too prim and proper for such an undertaking. I love her all the same; she reminds me of her mother, my aunt Myrtha, whose presence always introduced some balance into my chaotic life.

In the end it seemed fitting to choose Children's Day as the occasion to celebrate my epic quest. I'm so pleased to have such fine company to mark the special day too: there are twelve of us in all, mostly friends from evening school. I'm more than prepared for the adventure, with two cameras (one mine and the other borrowed), marker pens for graffiti, an aluminium flask full of water, and a copy of the Wayfarer's Prayer, just to ensure everything goes well. We arrive at Plaza de la República by our own means (no need for that pick-up!) at eleven o'clock in the morning on a cold and beautiful sunny Sunday of August.

As soon as my giant friend comes into view, I salute him

and tell him I've brought him some visitors. He may find it a little inappropriate to turn up like this without any warning and with so many people, but I'm sure my friend the Obelisk will understand.

Even before we arrive at the door, we can already see a blue patrol car from the Federal Police parked up nearby; within five minutes a van from the Municipality of the City of Buenos Aires appears and parks up right at the foot of the monument. There's no sign of any ambulances though! A man wearing work clothes steps out of the van and promptly asks us, "Which of you is Esteban?"
"I am", I answer, raising my right arm purposefully.
"And who's going up?"
"All of us, *señor*", I reply in a self-assured tone.
"Well then, I guess we better get going".

The municipal worker heads straight over to the strong iron door of the Obelisk and pulls out of his right pocket that same key that was mine for several days. He then pauses a moment, looks me square in the eye and says, "Director González expressly ordered me to allow you, Esteban, to open the door and go up first". My face beams with pride as he hands me the key.

Without further delay, I insert it into the little hole under the doorknob and turn it to the left not once, not twice, but thrice, and the door opens to total darkness. I swiftly step into the blackness followed by eleven other sets of curious eyes which, like mine I'm sure, are trying to pierce with undisguised wonder the great grim hollow before them. A cold silence suffused with fear suddenly takes hold of us.

No one dares say a word. All of us are gasping, bewildered, as our eyes slowly adjust. There's no elevator or escalator, not even a spiral staircase; just a wide hole above our heads with a long vertical tunnel stretching upwards, at the top of which, far away, you can make out a vague light coming in through a little square.

A particular smell hangs in the air, one of enclosure compounded by damp and foul air.

On the floor there's a metal grid from which a warm breeze blows up from time to time. Our first fright comes all of a sudden when a train passes underneath us at speed producing a thunderous din, a flash of light, and a rush of hot air that shoots out, enveloping us all, brushing over our skin as if it were the breath of the Obelisk himself.

I breathe in deeply. Glancing around me once more to assess my surroundings, I now feel confident to take charge of the expedition. To my left, fixed to the wall, I see a walking elevator, I mean a thin ladder with a seemingly countless number of iron rungs. It appears to be the only way up. I once again go first, followed close behind by my eleven sidekicks, one by one. There's no going back now either. I start to feel slightly underprepared: no gloves, no helmet, no hooks and no safety ropes! We're armed only with heaps of energy and a desire for conquest…

As I don't have any trainers, I'm wearing a pair of rope-soled espadrilles. The iron steps soon make my feet ache but I keep on, up and up, counting the steps as I go. Every ten meters or so, there's a small cement platform (there are seven in total) where I pause briefly to catch my breath. Standing there looking down sure gives me vertigo but it doesn't take anything away from the intense feeling of happiness.

I return to the task at hand. I can now feel on my face another type of air, much cleaner, purer and fresher. I remember my old school headmistress Elena and my first visit to the city and I picture her staring at me in surprise, her eyes wide open like a pair of mothballs.

I remember the great ignominy I felt in front of my classmates, the weeping that drenched my whole being from the inside, humiliated as I was by my own ignorance. Up a few more steps. The more intense the pain grows in the soles of the feet, the more joy overflows from my heart. After another two rests, I'm almost at the top. I can see the sunlight straining through the four tiny little windows. Only a few more meters to go and then I find myself on the last step, number 206. Here I am. At the top of the Obelisk. I finally did it!

All I find there is a small room, about three metres by three, each side with its little window, in the middle of which is a pulley for hauling up who knows what materials. Fast behind me come the others, one by one: those who believed in me, those who doubted me, and those who right up to the very last moment laughed and mocked but nonetheless came.

Sitting in the windows of the Obelisk, wearing a red jumper, I'm easily visible to the police who are looking out for us far below in the Plaza. I can also see other people waving at me and return their greetings waving my hand, so overcome with emotion that I start to cry. Generally speaking, people are never whole-heartedly content with life, at any given moment, but today I can genuinely say that my joy is overflowing.

From up here, the city looks totally different from the one I know. Only a few muffled noises reach my ears through the breeze while I watch the coming and going of hundreds of cars, all different shapes and colours.

Thus I achieve my long-awaited dream, here inside the head of my dear friend, the Obelisk. In doing so, I'm able to recover, through perseverance, patience and courage, my lost self-esteem.

I take a black marker out of my trouser pocket and scribble on the inner wall that faces east: "You have to learn a lot to understand that all you really need to learn is how to understand". It's just that no one fully appreciates why I needed to go up the Obelisk.

Reflecting on my life, from the shoulder of this giant, looking out to the eastern horizon, I dream of future conquests. I promise myself to keep studying, to finish secondary school at all cost and then attend a good university. I want to complete at least two university degrees, learn several languages, travel the world (starting in Israel), plant trees, and build a proper home for my mum and another for me. I vow not to let anyone humiliate me ever again. I decide there and then to walk away from ignorance and poverty, in search of a life of peace; I want to one day buy a typing machine to write a book and strive to be happy. Could I ever succeed? What it does mean to be happy?

CHAPTER SIXTEEN
Lidia
Patient and mentor

Walking past a travel agency one day, I spot an ad in the display window for Hotel El Conquistador, located on Suipacha between the streets Paraguay and Marcelo Torcuato de Alvear. The sleek design of the poster instantly catches my eye, as does the slogan splashed across it, to an even greater extent; together they awake in me an almost ineluctable desire to venture into the world of hospitality.

Without thinking twice I make my way to said hotel and who do I find standing at reception but the famous Uruguayan writer, Mario Benedetti, a brown poncho covering his shoulders. I recognise him only as our eyes meet and raise my eyebrows by way of a greeting, then address him, "Good afternoon, Sr. Benedetti, I'm an admiring *leedor* of your work *Tales and Nostalgias*".
"Aha. I see that you're also a *leedor* of Don Quixote", he says. Then he asks "And what do you think of my book?"
"I'm really enjoying it actually, though it does make me a little gloomy", I reply.
"But that is precisely the art of writing, young man: to alter our mood when we're confronted by the written word", he retorts.
"Sr. Benedetti, you're the only writer I like who has a moustache".
At this he roars with laughter, and is joined in his mirth by the receptionist, who's been listening along to our conversation, up until now discreetly.

I notice a pin on the left side of her brown uniform, half

obscured by abundant locks of curly hair, on which I can just about make out the name 'Lidia'.

"Srta. Lidia, good afternoon. I'd like to speak to the manager, please", I tell her resolutely.

"He's called Sr. Ketzner and he's in his office right over there", she replies promptly, indicating the office door with her hand. I thank her, take a deep breath to fill me with courage and walk over to knock on the door.

"Come in", he mutters, and then looks at me inquiringly. As I take in his features, I can't help but be reminded of that wonderful comedian and thinker, Tato Bores. I introduce myself and promptly express my wish to venture into the world of hospitality, telling him I've just come across a promotional poster for the hotel. I mention the phrase that drew me in: "Bring your dream to life, come and stay in El Conquistador".

Sr. Ketzner smiles and says, "Ah, I'm glad you liked it. It's a phrase I actually came up with", he pauses, quite pleased with himself, "Now, you said you want to venture into hospitality, why's that?"

"Well, I've been working as an office boy in several places for quite a while now and I'm looking to change things up a bit".

"Are you studying?"

"Yes, I'm currently completing my secondary education at an evening school".

"Do you speak any other languages?"

"Yes: English and Italian; I'm also studying Hebrew."

"Where's that?"

"In the AMIA[1]".

"And why are you studying Hebrew?"

"Because, forgive me, but my dream is not in fact to stay in Hotel El Conquistador; from a young age I have dreamed of travelling the world, and I'd like to start in Israel".

"Very well. How would you like to be our new hotel *groom*?"

"What's that?"

"It's like an errand boy, or a bellboy of sorts, actually a step below a bellboy. It's basically someone who works alongside the concierge as a helper, in charge of taking messages either coming in by phone or those left at reception. You'd be responsible for delivering them to the guests. You have to put each message in an envelope with the recipient's name on the front, written in clear handwriting, and slide it under the door of that guest's room. Being a hotel *groom* requires being on your feet a lot of the time, moving around. You can take the elevator up, of course, but to get down you'll have to use the stairs".

He goes on to tell me that I'll need to pay constant attention to the guests and remember that they're not my friends; that I'll have to keep my distance, stay at least *a hundred centimetres* from them and, if possible, avoid looking them in the eye; that, if I'm to do it, I must be extremely punctual, never lie nor make any mistakes. Above all, he insists that a *groom* in a guest room does not hear or see a thing, that they are discreet at all times, that they listen only for orders. "Are you up for it?" he says, finally.

"I'm ready, one hundred percent, Sr. Ketzner".

---

1   Asociación Mutual Israelita Argentina

Thus I leave behind the world of accounting and begin my foray into that of hospitality.

I learn a lot every day at Hotel El Conquistador as I'm dealing with guests from all over the world, all concentrated in a single building. I also start receiving tips, many of them in US dollars: they'll be very handy for the trip I'm planning…

After a few months I'm promoted from *groom* to bellboy, which means I start spending my days standing to one side of the entrance, facing another bellboy, chatting away discreetly, almost stiff in the legs, telling the odd joke, but always attentive to the comings and goings of the guests, opening the door for them and helping them with their luggage, always with a smile and a '*Buenos días* or *buenas tardes señor* or *señora*'.

The famed Boca Juniors begin staying at the hotel on Thursdays. Each player is given a double room so that they can focus on the weekend match ahead. Among them is of course their main star, an absolute machine of Argentine football, who goes by the name of Diego Armando Maradona. He's in the middle of his great epiphany and already well known around the country. He dazzles with his speed, his masterly control of the ball. Not only do I recognise him having watched him play on TV, but the image of his face has stayed with me ever since I saw an interview he gave to a journalist called Papaleo. Maradona was still a kid at the time, about twelve years old, very poor just like I was. When Papaleo asks him what he wants to be when he grows up, he candidly replies, "I want to be a good footballer. I want to play in a *Mundial*".

This answer from Maradona, so young and poor, living in Villa Fiorito, continues to inspire me for the rest of my life. I too want to be the good player; not in football, but in life. I want to be *mundial*, world-wide and world-wise. I was as poor as he was a few years ago, but through hard work and perseverance I'm slowly managing to escape from poverty, and now I'm working and studying full-time.

When I see Maradona himself stepping off a white bus along with the whole Boca Juniors squad, I quickly ready myself to help him with his bag. My fellow bellboy knows exactly what I'm up to, however, and turns to me asking, "What are you doing, man? Can't you see the players are taking their own bags? Remember you have to keep your distance with the guests".

That one-metre distance sometimes seems like an abyss to us staff members, but with Maradona, there's something different at work; Diego feels very familiar. He acts like I do.

I hear my fellow bellboy say something else, but I'm not listening any more. My eyes are fixed, expectantly, on Maradona. I wait a few seconds more and then brazenly step out to meet him, an offer twitching on my lips. I look for a moment into his lively eyes and then ask him, "May I take your bag, *señor*?"

He stares back at me with a broad smile and says, "No, no need to, *petiso*, I've got it, thanks".

I shake off the disappointment and begin patiently waiting for next Thursday to come around, for the same situation to arise, at that very same time. The white bus arrives like clockwork and, again, I stride forward to offer my humble services to Maradona. He sees me coming and, again, looking me in the eye, says, "No, thank you, *petiso*, I'll take it. But, here, have a sweet".

I'm more than happy to settle for that! He hands me a small round black sweet called *Media Hora* and I pop it straight in my mouth; maybe it's down to my excitement, but as soon as this little ball comes into contact with my saliva it slips right down the back of my throat, causing me to choke momentarily.

Diego looks at me surprised and bursts out laughing. But it's not long before he digs back into his pocket and produces another *Media Hora*, smiling at me without saying a word.

These are precisely my favourite sweets, of course; there's something so morish about that blend of anise and fennel. According to their name, they're supposed to last for 'half an hour' in the mouth, but this isn't technically true; I've found they last a maximum of twelve minutes, and that's at a normal sucking rate. I know this because I've timed myself before and tell him so. Diego listens but makes no reply.

The following week, the same situation is repeated, only this time he asks me my name.

"Esteban *Dido*", I reply, making a silly pun with '*este bandido*' (this bandit).

He lets out a little chuckle and then replies, "Diego Armando", looking at me with his kindly eyes, and then, placing his hand lightly on my shoulder, he gives me a kiss on the cheek.

This rapport with Diego has the other bellboys in fits of jealousy but, oh well, what can I do if he chose me? Or did I choose him perhaps? I don't know or care!

The Boca team rolls in to the hotel almost every week during the league season and every time it does I await Diego's hug, kiss and *Media Hora* sweets. As time goes on, I no longer let him get away with calling me *petiso* ('shorty') without some playful retort. "Look who's talking!" I say to him one day, "I'm *shorty*?! What does that make you then?"

Hearing this his face lights up with surprise: he and I are exactly the same height, of course.

He smiles and puts his arm around me. I notice how every time I see him he always seems to be eating sweets; sweets which no longer come my way in ones and twos, but whole handfuls, and not just *Media Horas* either, but chewy fruity ones too.

For the next six months I continue waiting for Maradona every Thursday, but he no longer comes; with the end of the league comes the end of his stays here at Hotel El Conquistador.

My daily commute involves taking the Bartolomé Mitre

train from San Isidro to Retiro, whereupon I set off to the Conquistador on foot. As I leave the train station the Sheraton Hotel looms into view on the other side of Plaza de Los Ingleses. It's a really huge building whose majesty I find endlessly captivating.

Susana Giménez, a national TV star, refers to the Sheraton on her show as the 'big white elephant' because sections of it have been left unfinished. She says it could well be converted into a huge hospital instead of being the first five-star hotel in the Argentine Republic.

In any case, the seed of a new desire begins to germinate inside me. One thing's for sure: to continue working at Hotel El Conquistador without Maradona there no longer makes sense to me. The days pass and my desire grows into an obsession, its roots reaching deep down into my very being.

I can even picture myself working there, boasting an elegant uniform, serving guests from all over the world of an altogether different class to those I meet at my current station.

In addition to Argentine australes, U.S. and Australian dollars, I imagine receiving my tips in Japanese yen, Spanish pesetas, French and Swiss francs, Chilean escudos, Israeli shekels, beautiful Brazilian cruzeiros, Greek drachmas, Italian lire and German marks. Indeed, I can already see myself saving up all these colourful foreign currencies in order to pay for my eventual passage to Israel. The weeks pass and I tell myself that the time has come to act. I can no longer simply dream of working in the big white elephant, I must do something to make it happen once and for all. My greatest longing is in fact to work for a company from the United States, since Mirtha Legrand said during one of her lunches that Americans are geared towards achievement and work extremely hard, in a relentlessly competitive manner.

I want to be like them, always active; sitting around doing nothing just seems like a complete waste of time. I think I'll learn a lot if I can get a job at the Sheraton Hotel.

I leave the house a little earlier today, resolute in my purpose, my thoughts fixed on that towering white elephant of a building as the city starts to flash by me on my usual route in to Retiro. This time when leaving the station, I make straight for the building opposite, with confident strides, in my finest clothes, my hair gelled and carefully combed.

As I approach the entrance, I'm greeted by a young-faced giant of a doorman called Alejandro, dressed in a grey suit with tails, a wonderful pink tie around his neck and a black top hat on his head that makes him look even taller than he already is. He opens the glass door for me announcing, "Welcome, sir!"
"Thank you", I reply, also in English, and then head over to a counter with a sign saying 'Conserjería' and address the

man there, "Good morning, *señor*, I'm here to see the shift manager".

"Would that be Sr. Santiago Castellanos?" He asks.

"Precisely", I respond, without flinching.

Of course, I have no idea who the shift manager is, but I nod in affirmation as if to suggest we have some prearranged meeting.

"He's currently having his morning coffee in the hotel cafeteria. Please, follow me".

As this man is escorting me, somewhat unhelpfully, to the unsuspecting shift manager, just as we're about to reach the area, the bell at the concierge desk rings out, brief and shrill, demanding his presence, to which he exclaims, "Sorry, I must get back, I'm being called upon, but look over there, that's Sr. Castellanos, the gentleman sitting near the window dressed in grey".

"Ah, yes, of course. Don't worry, I'll manage from here. Many thanks, *señor*".

The concierge's departure puts me at ease again and I walk over to the table indicated where there sits a tall thin man, in his sixties perhaps, slightly bald, peering through his glasses at a copy of *La Nación* and occasionally sipping at a cup of freshly brewed coffee.

I take a customary deep breath for courage and enquire, "Sr. Santiago Castellanos?"

"That's me", he replies, in a pure Castilian accent, reminiscent of Don Justo, the electrician who fled Franco's dictatorship and installed electricity in our shack.

"Esteban Cichello Hübner", I introduce myself, sticking out my right hand.

He readily shakes it while looking me fully in the eye in a display of charisma and honesty.

"Well, Sr. Esteban, what brings you here?"

"I have come to offer you the best of my experience in hospitality in the hope that there might be a part to play for me in the wonderful world of the Sheraton".

"Your experience?" He pauses for a moment, before saying, "Please sit, I'd be glad to hear more".

I slowly sit down opposite him and proudly announce, "I'm a professional bellboy, working at Hotel El Conquistador, the finest employee in the whole establishment".

"And how do you know you're the best?"

"Well, I'd say, judging from the tips I receive and the comments by the guests, there's no doubt I'm the best".

Seeing his lips curl into a smile, I continue by telling him that on my way to work each day, as I leave Retiro station, I always take a longing look at the Sheraton and picture myself working there.

"Would you be willing to give me a chance?" I ask.

At this, he stretches his long neck down to one side and takes a glance under the table, returning to the upright position before saying, "I see your shoes are spotless, young man, worthy in fact of someone who wishes to work for the Sheraton Hotel Group. I might add that you have also arrived at just the right time: only this morning I received an internal memo stating the need for another member at the concierge desk".

For a moment, while continuing to listen, I take note of this man's shrewd observation. It's true I always walk in well-polished shoes; this compensates for the holes in their soles and the cotton-fillers I stuff inside their tips so I don't end up sliding around too much. They're far too big for me of course, which is often the problem with hand-me-down presents.

"Well, Sr. Castellanos, here I am… and I want that position", I tell him with a determined voice.

"Very well then, take my card and go see the staff manager. He will decide if you fit the profile".

I thank him very much and shake his hand again, assuring him he won't regret giving me this opportunity. I then wonder to myself whether I am indeed the type of person they're after… Why do we create people profiles?

CHAPTER SEVENTEEN
Nina
Eccentric and avant-garde

When my new post is sufficiently secured I stand down from my role at the Hotel El Conquistador and begin my conquest of the White Elephant. My colleagues, including the general manager Sr. Ketzner, organise a farewell party for me in the hotel basement involving cake and soft drinks. They all express joy for my new beginning, particularly the receptionist Lidia Leninberg, who's become a true friend and mentor to me.

She has always supported me in many ways and would often help me with homework for my Hebrew classes. There are others there, however, who cannot hide their jealousy; two or three even express relief at my departure because of how many tips I used to make as well as all the praise the guests would shower upon me.

The Sheraton Hotel fast becomes something of an intensive course on interpersonal relationships, studied through a myriad of discoveries and adventures; where you have to look sharp, smile and act in the proper manner at all times. Such flawlessness in appearance greatly intensifies any pain forced under the surface. Politeness, silence and discretion are valued above all other things.

I start out at the concierge desk paying my dues as a *groom*, running errands and messages to and from the rooms. The hotel has 900 rooms and a permanent flow of communication that doesn't allow for any dawdling whatsoever on my part.

Control of this exchange centres around the telephone switchboard where four operators are frantically and relentlessly taking down messages for the guests. First, they write the note on a special form using carbonic paper, then put the original in an envelope for me to deliver to the guest and keep the spare copy in a file.

There's a large board in this room on which each hotel room is marked by a small aluminium tags where you can find the name and surname of the guest, their days of arrival and departure, the rate they're paying and other important details such as: VIP, company name, do not disturb, discretion required, or some other relevant observation. The little tags are arranged in two ways: one in alphabetical order by the surname of each guest and the other in numerical order, according to each room respectively. The same scheme can be found at reception behind an enormous counter where a host of receptionists shuffle back and forth with robotic productivity and permanent smiles. It's here that I quickly befriend Mariano Pérez, James Buchanan and Ricardo Dominguez; all three of them are bright, efficient and speak several foreign languages.

My uniform consists of a grey three-piece suit, a white shirt, blue tie and black shoes. It comes as no surprise that delivering messages is absolutely exhausting. Just like I often did at El Conquistador Hotel, I take the elevator to the top floor and then go down the stairs floor by floor, all 24 of them, knocking on doors to deliver the messages by hand if possible—waiting a few extra seconds occasionally renders a tip—and if there's no answer, I slide the envelope under the door.

I've noticed there are various airline crews who come to stay at the Sheraton, among them are Lufthansa, Air France, Varig, Alitalia, KLM, Iberia, Pan-Am, SAS, but my favourite is the Aeroflot crew from the USSR.

The crew members of this communist-run company usually arrive together and always appear somewhat frightened; one can tell immediately they have limited freedom of movement here. I don't know why but they do not wear perfume at all. They enter the hotel with grave looking faces, lining up two by two to check in to their rooms as if a well-drilled unit in the Red Army. They view everything around them with a certain distrust and are the only crew not to take single rooms for each member, opting instead to share twin rooms. When I ask at the concierge desk why this is so, the chief concierge, Sr. Pereyra, explains to me that it's because they're Soviet communists and have to keep one another in check so that neither can run off to live in some capitalist and free democracy.

They usually stay for a week at the hotel before returning to Moscow. Gosh, I'd love to visit Moscow one day! I believe I just may, too… and when I'm there, I'll be sure to make a trip to Leningrad; they say it's a stunning city, with its famous *Hermitage* museum, which means 'refuge for a hermit' and contains more than three million works of art.

Now it's final: I promise myself to go there someday.

The morning after their first night with us, the whole Aeroflot crew tend to step out into *Plaza de los Ingleses* to take a group photo in front of the tower before quickly returning to the hotel.
Following close behind them are mysterious Soviet security agents whose only responsibility is to guard the crew members; they aren't even able to go for a walk in San Telmo or down Calle Florida, let alone enjoy the city at night, going out for some tango or visiting a brothel, like other airline crews tend to do.

One day there was huge uproar at the hotel following the disappearance of the captain and co-pilot of an Aeroflot crew. After casually going over to the hotel safety deposit boxes and removing all their belongings, they stealthily vanished, defecting not only from the airline, but also the Soviet Union itself.

A colleague of mine mentions there are rumours they took a bus to the border province of Misiones, from where they could no doubt cross clandestinely into Brazil to finally relish their longed-for freedom and a sense of safety in that vast and wonderful country.
Unfortunately for the rest of the crew, this time they couldn't get back home and had to wait another week at the Sheraton for a new crew to arrive from Moscow with an extra captain and co-pilot onboard. I must say I'm very pleased for the escapees: I can picture them celebrating

their freedom between shots of Smirnoff or ice-cold Caipirinhas on some tropical beach of the Brazilian coastline; it's a thought that makes me laugh with delight as I try to remember their faces.

The months trickle by and I quickly tire of my role as *groom*; the new goal I've set myself is to become a receptionist, but I'm also well aware I still have much to learn about the inner workings of the hotel and must first gain some more insight. I turn to Sr. Pereyra one day and ask him to promote me to bellboy.

"Esteban, I've had my eye on you", he replies, "You're pretty alert, it's true, but to be a bellboy you have to be strong too. The suitcases are heavy. Do you think you're capable of lifting them?"

"I can assure you, Sr. Pereyra, though I appear short and skinny, I'm as strong as a donkey. Just you wait".

He lets out a laugh and then decides to give me a go. That's how I start my life as a bellboy at the Sheraton Hotel in Buenos Aires. Gradually the other bellboys come to accept me. They're quite a jealous bunch, whether that concerns my work rate, tips or even dealings with the guests; I think they just find it difficult to welcome another member into their team, especially one so young. What's more, they're more than a little miffed that my English is better than theirs and they tell me so, unreservedly.

During my holidays from evening school, I request to be given some night shifts as well, which last from 10p.m. to 7a.m. As there isn't a great deal to do at night, it's considered quite a unique shift, one which presents a wonderful opportunity to make mischief…

It also happens to be at a time when the 18th, 19th and 20th floors have just been refurbished. The room renovations included a change in carpets that required a two-centimetre margin at the foot of the doors, thereby allowing for the new lavish matting.

It is precisely on these floors that Napoleon Córdova, the reception manager, decides to put the numerous newly-wed couples who come to the hotel to spend their wedding night. It's part of something called a *Paquete de Luna de Miel* (Honey Moon Package). Another bellboy and friend of mine called Amilcar introduces me to a fun game that has me instantly hooked and increasingly committed. Put simply, we pay these special rooms a visit, usually about thirty minutes after they've gone up themselves. They tend to arrive in the early hours of the morning, around 3 or 4, after their respective wedding parties. Many of them are doubtless intoxicated with happiness and brimming with untold desires to realise, once and for all, their carnal union within the holiness of marriage.

We go into the corridors and crouch in front of the rooms with small rectangular mirrors that we slide under the doors like envelopes. Pressing down with the mirrors on the plush carpets we secure a clear and exclusive view of the activity inside in the room. The scenes I watch unfolding in the supple hotel beds are both nourishment and contribution to my teenage loneliness.

As a bellboy, I'm now charged with taking the guests' suitcases up to their rooms, or down to the lobby, on a four-wheeled trolley. I'm also the one who has to deliver an endless quantity of gifts and bouquets throughout the hotel.

One day, my trolley loaded with a number of bouquets, I notice a particularly large and beautiful one that's destined for the presidential suite, usually reserved for VIP guests, the wealthiest and most important or famous people staying with us. As I go to drop it off, I find, to my surprise, there's no usual guard sitting outside the suite. I ring the doorbell and, almost immediately, an eye flashes across the peephole; then the door is swiftly opened and a man suddenly stands before me to accept the flowers inside. His cautious expression changes in an instant to reveal a fresh, smiling face. I notice him reading the name written on the badge over my left breast pocket and, after a short pause, he says to me with an utterly mellifluous voice, "Please wait a second".

My heartbeat starts to quicken. He closes the door and, after a few seconds, no more, he reopens it and places thirty dollars in my hand, and closing them between his tells me: "Thank you",

"No, thank youuuuuuuu", I reply, mimicking his sing-song tone.

"How do you pronounce your name by the way?" He then asks me.

"ES-TE-BAN", I say, very slowly, before turning the

question back on him with my proud English accent, "And what is your name, sir?"

"My name is Frank", he says, "Frank SI-NA-TRA".

I flush red with glee and smile with every muscle in my face. What's more, I have another thirty dollars for my trip to Israel!

After some time, Sr. Napoleon Córdova this time calls me into his office for a meeting. He interviews me in English knowing that, having come from El Conquistador Hotel and worked for a few months at the concierge desk of the Sheraton, I'm quite proficient at it now. His offer is for me to move to reception, on condition that I do a few weeks training in the Reservations and Telephone Switchboard department; it's a position that, if I get things right, will lead me to the coveted *Front Desk*. I accept the challenge with relish.

This internship of sorts makes me fall even more in love with the hospitality sector. I realise how much I like the people in it, the guests from all over the world, each of them with their fears, their differences and disparate social backgrounds, all carrying that same heavy pack on their backs for the simple fact of being human beings. In the Telephone Switchboard room, one of the things I enjoy doing is executing wake-up call requests and greeting the guests with a 'Good morning, Mr. So-and-so, it's seven o'clock'. One of the first clients to ask me to wake him up, after a pitiful four-hour rest, is the President of Peru Alan García. I'm quite nervous before calling but decide to rip up the rulebook on this occasion and wish him a wonderful and productive day.

The hotel is actually planning to replace this wake-up call system with a device they call a computer, which will call the guests automatically and without fail. Though totally efficient I'm sure, this idea doesn't appeal to me in the slightest as I feel the human touch will make all the difference between us and the future talking machines.

After a month of training I'm finally promoted and given my long-awaited receptionist uniform: a new white shirt, a bordeaux coloured blazer with matching tie, grey trousers and black shoes.

The front desk at the Sheraton Hotel is a fabulous setting for me. But, when I'm *backstage*, in the office behind the scenes, I often find myself quite solemnly reflecting on all the troubles in my personal life, on all the needs that my mother and siblings still have, on her toxic relationship with an increasingly alcoholic and abusive husband who beats her frequently and then threatens her with his suicide. I think about how I don't have enough money and about how, now I'm a receptionist, I'm going to have a slightly higher salary but at the same time I'm going to lose out on the tips that bellboys usually make.

Little by little I endear myself to my new colleagues at reception, while continuing to learn lots from them all the time. They're truly admirable professionals on the hotel stage.

Today we have Topo Gigio coming to stay, that friendly Italian mouse known the world over. He's accompanied by his owner and maker, Maria Perego, and his Spanish dub voice, sweet and mellow, provided by the Uruguayan, Juan Carlos Mareco, followed by his costume manager and then his personal assistant, a kind, intelligent Hindu man named Rajiv Devi who claims to be an expert in levitation. I'm not sure what that's all about, but it's clear he speaks excellent Italian and English.

I soon find out that Topo Gigio isn't a single doll either, but many, and all identical. Being and speaking a little Italian myself, and being something of a charmer as well, like Gigio, I make friends with his entourage in no time, and it turns out they're staying for a whole week at the Sheraton too.

When the troop of *Gigio* finally come to check out one night, Giovanni the tailor shakes my hand goodbye and tells me he'd like to give me a tip but he's spent all his cash. He has some travellers checks left too, but since they're for personal use, he can't offer them either. Never mind, he has something better for me. He casually hands me a package weighing around two hundred grams, ten centimetres by five approximately. I politely decide not to open it in front of him and place it in the jacket pocket of my neat uniform, returning his smile and then thanking him emphatically for this unknown gift, "*Grazie, grazie. Non avrei dovuto. La ringrazio molto, ma non è necesario*".

"*Te lo meriti, Stefano*", he answers me, with a mischievous smile.

With the friendly band of Italians on their way to Ezeiza International Airport, I open the package and discover, to my great astonishment, what looks to me like compressed grass of a greyish-green colour. My colleagues at the front desk can tell from my expression I haven't a clue what this Italian tailor has just given me, so one of them, Mariano, pipes up, "Esteban, you lucky bugger, they gave you marihuana!"
"Mary what?" I ask, perplexed.
"*Macoña, cannabis sativa…*".
I'm still not sure what it is but I soon realise it's something illegal.

As the night shift wears on and activity at reception dies down, two by two the receptionists sneak off into the office of Sr. Napoleón Córdova himself, boss of the front desk, to smoke up the gift of Topo Gigio. The build up of fumes and intense smell of marihuana are totally new to me. Once lit, the *magnos canutos* (great big joints) create large white-grey clouds of smoke, giving the impression that a small fire has broken out here in the *backstage* of the hotel where, under the influence, we compete to see who can best imitate the voice of Topo Gigio. Although I certainly don't win this competition, it is the moment I stop having to pay my dues in the new role, a moment me and my great team of 'Sheratonian Stoner' receptionists can really cut loose together.

The world of hospitality continues to stimulate me every day. I go work full of enthusiasm and apply myself with real passion to everything I do. The CGT, *Central General de Trabajadores* (General Workers Union), has issued the call for another general strike tomorrow. As a response, the hotel management is sending round a memo today informing us all that employees who don't join the strike will be rewarded. Our reception team assembles to decide together what we're going to do. We vote unanimously in favour of rejecting the proposal and decide we all want to work instead. Furthermore, to avoid problems getting in to work tomorrow, we also decide to stay the night at the hotel. I can hardly contain my excitement: it's the first time I've ever slept in a five-star hotel! Who would've thought it…

The next day, I work the first half of the day as a waiter in the restaurant and the second half as an attendant cleaning rooms with the maids. In every team you can even find loyal guests volunteering to cover for the staff who've decided to go on strike. It feels quite special seeing everyone working together as one big family to keep our second home up and running.

All the excitement of the day is however marred by an unfortunate incident that takes place when I'm on duty at the VIP reception on the 24th floor. A German tourist with the surname Müller approaches me asking for the room number of an Aeroméxico air hostess called Sandra

Gabriela Espinosa Faneau.

"Sir", I try to explain to him at first, "the Aeroméxico crew doesn't stay with us".

"Yes, it does. That air stewardess is definitely here", he replies to me in broken Spanish, revealing a certain Germanic aggression in his voice.

"Let me just check. I should warn you, though, that if she is indeed staying here, for privacy reasons, I wouldn't be able to give you her room number", I tell him in a dry tone before adding, "I can only contact her by phone and then connect you to the call".

I then flick through the Sheraton & Towers register, but to no avail, so I call down to the main reception; nothing. All the while each one of my movements is being closely followed by the inquisitive gaze of this man, who, it is clear, is growing increasingly agitated. As a final attempt to end the vain search, exhausting all my means, I phone through to the switchboard operators. That should satisfy him. I can be quite sure the guest isn't here. I can sense, nevertheless, an unhappy turn coming my way, I feel it hanging in the air between us, a glimmering tension radiating from this angry inebriate, seeped in the sour stench of booze. Save for his heavy breathing, his frame remains quite still for a moment as he awaits my verdict.

"No, sir, I'm afraid Sra. Sandra Gabriela Espinosa Faneau is not staying at our hotel", I tell the German man.

"Ich bin mir ziemlich sicher, dass Sie hier ist!!!!" he screams at me, before suddenly grabbing me by the tie, pulling me tightly towards him, to the point that I'm actually choking, and repeating the same ghastly phrase

over and over.

As if this attempted murder isn't enough for him, he casts me down and then picks up the square television next to me, with even more violence, and hurls it against the window. I watch it smash straight through the glass and then disappear into the darkness. It plummets at a speed unimaginable to me before blasting through more panes of glass and finally laying to rest on the floor of the Golden Horn nightclub, 23 floors below.

All I can think is thank heavens I wasn't the one thrown through the window. Members of our security team eventually arrive and restrain the rampant guest by force. Once tempers have cooled, the hotel management orders the German man's company to cover the expenses of the damages caused, as well as offer me a monetary gift to make up for the shock he'd given me and for any further psychological damage the whole affair may have caused me. This compensation is invaluable to me as it helps pay for five of the eighteen installments on a plane ticket I've arranged to take me half way round the world. The irony of a violent German collaborating towards my trip to Israel gives me great pleasure.

Misfortune strikes again after we get a memo at the front desk informing us that the hotel has oversold rooms by mistake and that the receptionists should try to redirect two or three guests to other nearby hotels. Well then, while my colleagues are on dinner break together, a rather bizarre-looking woman appears at reception: her hair is all dishevelled, streaked in various colours, her face caked in make-up, she's wearing a black leather outfit and smoking a cigarette; she tells me her name is Hagen, that she has a reservation.

I welcome her, find her reservation, and discover she has booked a single room for a week, with no additional information. I apologise and explain that the hotel has unfortunately oversold its rooms and that we have nowhere for her to stay. She mutters a few foul profanities in German but insists no further and declares she'll go to the Plaza Hotel.

There's no cause for alarm until I spot a group of about twenty people enter, all with instruments, huge bags and hotel reservations. As they gather in front of the unusual guest I've just sent packing, my eyes nearly pop out of their sockets. She presently issues an order fitting of a commander addressing her troops. *"Wir sind hier nicht erwünscht, gehen wir zum Plaza Hotel!!!"* she bellows out. As much as I implore her to stay, telling her I've made a grave error, I'm unable to stop her and she leaves the hotel howling that her presence wasn't welcome in the Sheraton and that she and her twenty companions were leaving for the Plaza Hotel.

As a result of my blunder, the hotel loses several thousand dollars. I'm just so clueless about music; I mean, besides Sandro, Michael Jackson, Carlos Gardel and Mercedes

Sosa, I don't know who *anyone* is. The greatly-offended guest is of course Nina Hagen, known throughout the world as the 'Witch of Berlin'.

This incident nearly costs me my job. However, a saviour appears in the form of Don Santiago Castellanos, the manager who helped me to get hired. He rushes to my defence arguing that I technically acted in accordance with the directives issued in the memo by the Reservations Department; the problem was that they were very poorly explained. He insists that the reservations for the 'Witch of Berlin' were made individually and without the proper supplementary information, thereby showing that I couldn't have been aware I was dealing with a VIP nor that she was part of a group of twenty. What a relief: I'm able to narrowly escape dismissal from the Sheraton.

My life takes another unexpected turn when a visionary compatriot, hamburger entrepreneur now smitten with the snow, Don Tito Lowenstein, passes over the Andes in a helicopter one day, seeking out an ideal spot for a ski resort. He soon after decides to buy up a whole valley, a handful of mountains and a couple of hills in the province of Mendoza. In just a few months he opens a winter resort complex called Las Leñas, the largest of its kind in South America.

Lowenstein hires Sr. Castellanos as his general manager of the new complex. Castellanos in turn, before leaving his post at the Sheraton for good, holds a discreet meeting with a small group of receptionists and housekeepers, of which I am one. He offers us the chance to follow him to Las Leñas. The salary makes it a very tempting proposition; on top of that, we'll be given free board and lodging and won't have to cover our travel costs. He says everything we earn we can save because there'll be practically nowhere to spend our money once there. Consequently, we all submit our resignations, every one of us, the crème de la crème of the Sheraton Buenos Aires Hotel staff, and off we go to Mendoza, almost crossing the entire mountain range before stopping just short of the Chilean border.

The departure of all twelve of us is certainly a great loss for the White Elephant.

In Las Leñas, I work as receptionist at the Hotel Géminis, ten hours a day, making sure everything runs smoothly at the front desk, supervising the maids, answering the phone and taking messages for the guests. To inspire its menus, the resort hires a first-class Argentine chef by the name of Francis Mallman.

He trains the chefs of the other hotels in the resort right here in our kitchen. The wonderful thing about this is that he always needs a guinea pig to taste the delicacies being prepared under his supervision. Thus I become an avid taster of gourmet titbits, puddings being my speciality... I soon realise how easily I'm corrupted by a Mallmann *crème brulée*, *zuppa inglese* or *tiramisù*.

During down time we're allowed to ski for free all over the resort, an arrangement of which I take full advantage, opting for some hours of ski lessons on almost each of my days off. I get the hang of it pretty quickly and after a short time leave behind the green runs for blue ones.

One day I venture out and take a lift up to the highest peak of the valley, with steep slopes, narrow channels, moguls and rocks abounding. I'm well aware it's meant for only the most experienced skiers; however, my unconscious propels me to take the risk.

Off I set down a black run, the so-called death run, and no sooner have I begun than I'm hurtling down the slope. I suddenly find myself alone on the mountain side going full tilt when, out of nowhere, I notice a great rock slumped in my path. There's no time for evasive action and I'm sent rocketing into the air more than thirty meters, my skis abandoning me mid-flight, before plunging headfirst into a heap of pristine snow. My whole body is bent over double, fully submerged in the snow. I'm left motionless and unconscious, head down and feet covered by a metre or more of snow. I've no idea how long I spend in this position, but when I do wake up I have the sensation I'm drowning; with my eyes closed I can see a light awakening me. But I can't move. At this moment, grandma Rachel drifts into my head and I imagine her body bent into a comma after that car crashed into her on Avenida Márquez back in San Isidro. I start to feel jolts through my body that aren't coming, I don't suppose, from any signals in my own brain. Yet the jolts grow in persistence and intensity until I'm finally able to free myself and, using my hands to support me, return to the surface and the sky.

Only now does the magnitude of the accident I've just had sink in and I begin to conceive of the idea that a higher force, the angel Mihael, perhaps, or luck itself, has saved me from death. I cry out inconsolably, thanking the heavens for having mercifully returned my soul to my body; I'm so grateful to be alive and for the most part unscathed. I return to the base on foot wondering how long the aches will last in my body and the great feeling of joy in my mind. I don't tell anyone what's happened. This is the last time I ever skied in my life.

Even today I still wonder if skiing is like cycling, or if you forget how to do it when you haven't practiced it for a long time.

Back at work in Las Leñas, a strong rivalry is developing between 'the twelve apostles', as we the Sheratonian team from Buenos Aires are known, and the local employees from Mendoza; but even greater still is the tension arising with the Chileans working in the ski centre.

Despite our differences, everything manages to stay on track until one day, one of the apostles, Ricardo, is falsely accused of providing certain services to a female guest that are not permitted. The staff manager, a *mendocino*, intends to fire him. Don Santiago Castellanos, our mentor and the manager of the whole hotel complex, on the other hand, defends him by employing an old *gallegada* ('*castilianism*') that goes, "What happens in Pucela stays in Pucela". They argue about it back and forth and finally decide to suspend him.

As it's only a few days to go until the start of world ski championships, it occurs to me to challenge the resort authorities by organising a general strike on account of the injustice suffered by my friend Ricardo. I create a couple of pamphlets and make 365 copies using the hotel photocopier. I begin handing them out to each and every employee in the resort but when the staff manager gets wind of my little scheme they suspend me too.

My suspension entails leaving Las Leñas for a week. I end up going to Malargüe to stay in a godforsaken dump. The only good thing is that my hovel of a hotel has a hot spring with water that, though reeking of rotten eggs, helps me endure the profound boredom I encounter. All I can do is soak in the sulphurous hot water while mulling over my future.

There is, however, one moment of wonderful excitement to punctuate the tedium: on the June 29th 1986, Argentina wins the World Cup in the great Estadio Azteca of Mexico City, beating the Federal Republic of Germany by three goals to two.

With the game tied and tensions rising, the brilliant Diego Maradona carves a masterful pass through to Jorge Burruchaga who runs clear and scores the decisive goal. Watching the game from the hotel, I leap for joy and at the same time burst into tears.

After the game they show the ongoing celebrations throughout the country, with thousands of people gathered in Plaza de la República where the figure of my friend the Obelisk stands proudly. Around his feet the revellers sing, dance and jump marking Argentina's second ever victory at the World Cup. I stare at the Obelisk and then picture in that very moment the euphoria of my other monumental friend, Diego Armando Maradona.

I'm fearful that the scars of my recent feud will re-open, that on my return to work in Las Leñas I'll be treated harshly. I'd like to tell all of them that people shouldn't be judged by their slip ups but by how many times they get back on their feet. I actually consider myself fortunate to have had a tough start to life because it has taught me how to keep getting back up.

I certainly don't regret organising a strike that failed. Having rid myself of my costume of guilt, I return to my post with head held high, proud to have defended a colleague in the face of my employers' injustice. I soon discover that all isn't as bad as previously feared either. As a result of my actions, my fame is surprisingly on the rise, a fact which actually helps to smooth things over between the three factions of Porteños, Mendocinos and Chilenos.

Our union is ultimately sealed when the resort is hit by a terrifying snowstorm one evening. It's so extreme in fact that the buses carrying tourists up and down the mountain are unable to operate; the one access route to the complex is completely blocked. We're stranded up here for a whole ghastly week and spend the entire first day just digging tunnels so we can get out of the hotels to the surface.

The terrible weather and bitter cold force us to spend time together that allows us to get to know each other better; as a consequence, our differences are soon forgotten.
What's new is that we have to start rationing food. Even if there's enough stored away for eventualities like this, we still don't know how much time we'll remain cut off from the outside world. Even helicopters can't get near us. We have to stay calm and be creative, entertaining the guests and keeping the mood cheerful so that panic isn't allowed to spread.

In other developments, skiing isn't the only first I can boast of in Las Leñas for I also have my first brush with romance at this time. Since there isn't much to do apart from work during the big snow dump, I try to make up for lost time.
The prevailing promiscuity really brings us all together and releases the tension between the rival groups of employees, thus liberating the lust from our hearts too.

During my time at Las Leñas, I'm able to save up enough money to finish paying for my ticket to Israel, and also to help my mum *and* take some extra money with me to spend in the Holy Land. Will it be enough? What is meant by abundant money?

CHAPTER EIGHTEEN
Raquel
Inspiring and remembered

269

I am ecstatic: I'm now holding in my hands the ticket for a fifteen-hour journey halfway round the world. I'll first be taking a KLM flight from Buenos Aires to Amsterdam's Schiphol Airport, and from there I'll board another plane, with El Al, to take me the rest of the way to Tel Aviv's Ben Gurion Airport.

Everything is ready for my destiny to change. We leave the house. We take a cab. I'm joined by my mother and a friend, Sarita Minyersky, both of a weepy disposition. On the way they give me an endless series of recommendations, that I do this and not that; I must visit Perla, take good care of my money, look out for terrorists, eat such and such a thing... They start crying, noses running like Río de la Plata, and, after hugging me over and over, they stand aside to watch me climb the boarding stairs. They don't once stop waving as I look back; it's as if they're going to stay in Buenos Aires Ministro Pistarini International Airport ready to wave their hands again as the plane takes off. That's just the way they are: mellow and loving. I can't believe I'm finally fulfilling my long-held dream of travelling to Israel.

I've wanted to leave Argentina for a while now, my beloved country, which has until now done me little good and given me plenty of misery, injustice and pain. Nonetheless, deep down, I firmly believe that my past misadventures in poverty are the greatest wealth I bring with me now to Israel.

My real thirst for Judaism is driven by my near-total ignorance of my heritage. My simple nature comes with a deep enthusiasm to learn more about the strange faraway land of Israel. I couldn't escape feeling so alienated, so detached, in the face of such treasure. This sense of estrangement only increased over the years as I thought about each passing generation of my family.

Now that I'm returning to my roots, I feel extremely anxious to find out more. I shan't miss an opportunity to receive wisdom, understanding and knowledge. I also know that prioritising my education will get me where I want to go.

The flight is unsurprisingly tedious but the energy I feel, and the happiness, is making it quite bearable.
Having said that, I am a little distressed by the misfortune of my seating placement, on row 32, right at the back of the plane. Just behind me is the smoking area and the smell of tobacco smoke penetrates my lungs and permeates all my clothes, so neatly prepared with all my mother's love.
The connecting flight from Amsterdam is a doddle in comparison, after enduring the tenacious security measures enforced by El Al, that is. I fare better with the seating plan this time and end up on row 18, on the window side, far from any nauseous fumes, ready to watch us touch down in the Promised Land.

There are many Orthodox Jews on the flight. Everything is quite quiet until a group of ten or so men, mostly bearded and each with a *kipa* on the crown of his head, begin their afternoon prayers, all standing up at the back of the plane, after which they take out several nine-branched candelabra called *hanukkiya* (*hanukkiyot* in plural) and place them on their tray tables.

They then light the third candle of Hanukkah on these *hanukkiyot* and the singing commences. I merrily join in with them as they share out *sufganiot*, jelly doughnuts, among the passengers in celebration of the victory of the Maccabees, 2,300 years ago… My thoughts quickly turn to my mum and to the only candles that she used to light at home whenever there was a power cut.

The joyful mood is suddenly interrupted when the stewardesses imperiously order the rabbis to blow out the candles they'd lit, reminding them of the potential hazards, at which point song gives way to uproar, pushing and shoving, and a coarse exchange in Hebrew that I can't quite make out. I don't quite know what's happening, but as the situation develops I'm continually amazed and amused in equal measure.

However, as the whole affair drags on, I'm left feeling a little confused, wondering whether Hanukkah is something happening now or whether it happened hundreds of years ago; whether the story of a small candle that warded off the ghastly gloom is itself now warding off human wickedness on this El Al flight, or bringing it ever closer… A flight attendant now has a fire extinguisher in her hands, pointed at a candelabrum, and is threatening action.

As a countermeasure, one of the rabbis is protecting the candelabrum with his body. The story of Hanukkah is still alive in those of us travelling on this flight, and surely on the outside too. You might say they put on one colossal cosmic drama in mid-flight to Israel. Who knows what's waiting for me there? Some want to bring light inside the plane, while others want darkness for the sake of safety.

It's surprising to think that Jews and ancient Greeks were able to understand each other to some extent when, here on this flight, Jews amongst themselves seem incapable of finding common ground. Both the Hellenes of antiquity and the Jews shared an appreciation for harmony; they valued wisdom and beauty, though it was the Jews who first came to recognise the only one great force behind the whole universe that is the basis of Jewish monotheism. Back then there was a certain harmony absent from this flight today.

The Jews of twenty-three centuries ago tolerated Greek domination until finally saying enough was enough, just as my new travel companions are saying enough to stewardesses who won't allow them to celebrate Hanukkah. It's a matter of rebellion again.
I ask someone to translate the discussion for me. One of the rabbis explains to me that El Al is a state-run company and therefore they have the right to celebrate a Jewish holiday in mid-flight.

Just as in the past when Antiochus forbade the Jews from observing Shabbat and studying Torah, so too today the irascible stewardesses wish to do the same by forbidding the celebration of Hanukkah.

This was how all-out war broke out on my first flight to Israel, similar to when, for the first time in history, it so happened that a people weren't fighting for their country or their lives, only to uphold their beliefs and preserve their right to religious freedom.

The problem was that, at the time, the Syrian-Greek army was the most powerful in the world; their soldiers had superior war strategies and they marched in a compact formation with their shields locked together. They also had more sophisticated weaponry, just like the stewardesses of El Al, armed with their fire extinguishers and syringes full of paralysis-inducing liquids, trained to deal with any adversity. It's clear that these well-equipped women constitute a far greater force than a handful of Orthodox Jews.

I carefully judge the situation and then ask myself that if it's acceptable for passengers to continuously light up matches for their cigarettes and smoking pipes throughout the flight, why are the stewardesses making such a fuss over a few small candles? Their flames are, after all, closely guarded by the joyous remembrance of the wondrous miracle that once illuminated the Great Temple of Jerusalem.

274

The image of this flickering candlelight evokes today the Maccabees who themselves believed that their victory had come from on high. When they finally recaptured the besieged city of Jerusalem, they sought and found a pot containing enough pure olive oil to light up the temple; the exact amount necessary to last a single day. Miraculously, however, the light of the *menorah*, that is, the candelabrum, burned for a full eight days, allowing enough time to make more oil.

It was a true miracle, the miracle of Hanukkah that we celebrate today on the plane, without permission. The discussion continues to grow ever more heated. It lasts for so long that when the flight captain eventually appears in an attempt to mediate the conflict, the candles no longer have any wax to burn, leaving only that pleasant aroma of freshly extinguished wicks wafting through the air.

Beside themselves, my companions take this as another sign from on high and begin to dance and sing once more. Soon the songs of Hanukkah have spread their infectious joy throughout the rest of the cabin and the faces of even the most secular-looking passengers are imbued with their spirit.

I come to the conclusion that there are miracles that happen every day, acts of simultaneity that we often call coincidence; yet if we open our eyes and pay attention we can see there really is no place on earth and beyond that is empty of the wonders of creation.

The flight attendants didn't exactly win the contest, but there aren't any more candles alight to jeopardise the flight either.

I start to see the funny side of this bizarre occurrence and find myself laughing out loud.

Shortly afterwards, Tel Aviv comes into sight through my little window. It's a truly breathtaking view and I'm suddenly struck by the thought of the thousands of soldiers who over millennia have given their lives for this land so that I could return today.

Upon arrival at Ben Gurion airport I find some delegates from the Agency awaiting me. They greet me warmly before taking me off to a hotel in the capital of Israel, Jerusalem.

My mum always told me as a child that Jerusalem had streets made of gold and a sea of crystal glass. I arrive in the Holy City well into the third night of the Festival of Lights and, with a mixture of enthusiasm and despair, pass through the Gate of the Tower of King David, also known as Jaffa Gate.

I enter the old town on the lookout for something special and walk with a sense of purpose down its narrow streets. The atmosphere is steeped in a peculiar sort of energy whose nature I've never before encountered. In fact, I think that even if you were blind, deaf and void of all smell, you would still easily recognise where you were, for Jerusalem is a city that makes the hearts of its visitors vibrate. She makes herself felt inside of you, in your soul.

I feel an unstoppable verve of energy racing through my chest, so intense it makes me want to cry. It is the chosen city, thrice-holy, where the earth meets the sky. It is sacred not only to Judaism, but also to Islam, with its revered Al-Aqsa mosque, and to Christianity, with its hill of Golgotha and the Holy Sepulchre.

It soon becomes apparent to me that the streets of Jerusalem are all built of a yellow like stone and not of gold as my mother had once told me. There is, however, something here that shimmers a little like gold, which is all around me: Jerusalemite stone. The 'sea' to which she referred I leave to one side, well aware there isn't one near Jerusalem; instead, I go in search of the *Kotel*, the Western Wall: the last vestige of the Holy Temple and, without doubt, the holiest place for the Jewish people. It is a place both public and also extremely personal where Jews and non-Jews alike pray with utter devotion.

I soon lose myself in this labyrinth of stone. When pausing to think, I'm unsure which way to turn. I find myself alone. There is no one to ask for help in the meandering alleyways going up and down, to the left and right. Nor does this worry me in any way for my feet seem to know exactly where they're taking me. I simply follow them, no doubts or hesitation, step by step, almost running, in fact, as I advance in my hungry search.

It begins to drizzle, an ethereal rain that caresses my skin and mixes delicately with the water of my soul; I can feel this blend now pouring down inside me over the seed planted long ago by my grandmother Raquel.

Facing so many great changes in flow and fortune over the years, the water of my soul now begins to emerge in the form of tears, tears so unimaginably beautiful and pure. Conjuring up this image, enraptured, my mind blots out all else until suddenly, before my baffled eyes, appears the great Western Wall, so often evoked in my dreams. It is all that remains of the retaining wall of the temple mount, where the very miracle of Hanukkah occurred, that same miracle that hours before we commemorated on the plane.

I presently take a *kipa* out of my pocket and place it on my head before running over to kiss this 'wailing' wall. I embrace it with my arms outstretched, weeping, and my heart battering against it, torn apart by fear. I can't fully grasp what I'm feeling but I recognise that it's something special, emanating from the depths of my soul. In one of the cracks separating these ancient stones I place the letter given to me by my mother, the contents of which I can't bring myself to read.

As my salty tears mingle with the sweet raindrops on my cheeks, promising me a fine blessing, I realise that while Jerusalem has no sea, I myself am an ocean of happiness.

I can't stop thinking about my mother and Grandmother. I picture their bone-weary hands wringing out ragged grey floor cloths back in the hospital of San Isidro. I think of all their deprivations, all the dreams they have had to sacrifice so that I myself could dream. They could live only with the fantasy of dreaming, a constant fantasy that helped them cope with the suffering they endured.

I thereby fulfil the greatest dream of my life, there, reverently facing the Holy Wall, trembling before its immense sanctity. In this instant I watch all the difficult moments and dark years of my past begin to transform; I notice doors once closed shut beginning to creak open, letting in glimmers of light as they do so.

In this instant my grandma Raquel keeps returning to my mind, as if nostalgically. She hands me a bunch of keys so that I can continue opening future doors. She looks at me full of love and longing, reciting to me one of her favourite verses:

"Tell me what strange reason brings forth those tears from you, my child, hanging like dew-curdled droplets from your trembling lashes?"

She comes back to life once more in me, so dearly missed, my dear Raquel. Today she lived again through me. Or was that yesterday?

The end

But this story continues…

Printed in Great Britain
by Amazon

15675594R00171